FOUR LECTURES ON MARXISM

FOUR LECTURES ON MARXISM

[PAUL M. SWEEZY]

MONTHLY REVIEW PRESS
NEW YORK AND LONDON

*For Sam, Lybess, Jeff, Moophy, Jenny,
and all their generation*

Copyright © 1981 by Paul M. Sweezy
All rights reserved

Library of Congress Cataloging in Publication Data
Sweezy, Paul Marlor, 1910–
  Four lectures on Marxism.
  Presented at Hosei University in Tokyo in the fall of 1979.
  Contents: Dialectics and metaphysics—The contradictions of capitalism—Center, periphery, and the crisis of the system—[etc.]
  1. Marxian economics—Addresses, essays, lectures.
I. Title.
HB97.5.S886   335.4   81-81694
ISBN 0-84345-583-X   AACR2
ISBN 0-84345-584-8 (pbk.)

Manufactured in the United States of America
10 9 8 7 6 5 4 3 2 1

[CONTENTS]

Preface   9

Lecture 1:
Dialectics and Metaphysics   11

Lecture 2:
The Contradictions of Capitalism   26

   Appendix A:
   The Law of the Falling Tendency
   of the Rate of Profit   46

   Appendix B:
   Competition and Monopoly   55

Lecture 3:
Center, Periphery,
   and the Crisis of the System   71

Lecture 4:
Marxism and the Future   85

[PREFACE]

The lectures on which this book is based were delivered at Hosei University in Tokyo in October 1979, on the announced subject of "Marxism Today." As explained at the beginning of the first lecture, my interpretation of this title was somewhat specialized, not to say idiosyncratic, and I think it would have been misleading to use it as the title of a book.

Hosei University celebrated its hundredth anniversary in 1980. During this whole stormy century of Japanese history, Hosei has been a leading center of humane scholarship and learning. I was therefore honored when its president, Mr. Akira Nakamura, and the Department of Economics invited me to give a series of lectures on Marxism, which is recognized in Japan, to a far greater extent than in my own country, as embodying and carrying on the finest traditions of Western philosophy and social science.

In working over the original texts of the lectures, I have benefited from suggestions, and even more from reassurances, from a number of friends, including Donald Harris, Professor of Economics at Stanford University; Teodor Shanin, Professor of Sociology at the University of Manchester; Samir Amin, until recently Director of the African Institute of Economic Development and Planning; Sol Adler, one of my fellow graduate students at the London School of Economics nearly fifty years ago who helped to introduce me to Marxism; and Harry Magdoff and Jules Geller, my colleagues at *Monthly Review* and Monthly Review Press. I have added two appendices to the second lecture on subjects which could not be encompassed within the lecture framework.

I owe a particular debt of gratitude to my good friend Tokue Shibata, now Professor of Economics at Tokyo Keizai University and formerly head of the Tokyo Metropolitan Research Institute for Environmental Protection. Professor Shibata handled all the arrangements for the visit to Japan and acted as a most gracious host while I was there.

—Paul M. Sweezy

New York City
May 1, 1981

[1]
DIALECTICS AND METAPHYSICS

The announced subject of these lectures is "Marxism Today," and I want at the outset to explain what it means to me as well as what it does not mean.

I am not going to attempt a survey, still less a critique, of the various schools and tendencies that consider themselves to be intellectual and/or political descendants of the founding fathers of Marxism, Karl Marx himself and Friedrich Engels. (I ought perhaps to add that in my view the differences between Marx and Engels were mostly matters of emphasis and formulation and as such are irrelevant to a discussion of Marxism of the kind I am proposing: to the limited extent that I feel the need for textual quotation, I shall draw on the writings of either one depending on which seems more appropriate to the point at issue.)

What I want to accomplish can perhaps be best clarified if I begin with a few autobiographical observations. I came to economics in particular and social science in general as a college student in the late 1920s. Harvard in those days had one of the more distinguished North American economics departments. It included, reading from left to right, institutionalists like William Z. Ripley, Marshallians like Frank W. Taussig, and dyed-in-the-wool conservatives like Thomas Nixon Carver and Charles J. Bullock. There were of course no Marxists on the Harvard faculty, and if there were any in the student body they were unknown to me. I do not recall Marx's name, let alone his ideas, ever being mentioned in any of the courses I took as an undergraduate. When I left Cambridge in 1932 for a year of graduate study at the London School of Economics, I had never been exposed to anything more radical than Thorstein Veblen's *Theory of the Leisure Class*, his most famous but far from his most radical book.

The year 1932-1933 proved to be a turning point in the history of the twentieth century. The prelude to World War II, if not the first act itself, was under way in the Japanese invasion of what was then called Manchuria. The Great Depression hit bottom in Western Europe and North America, giving rise to two simultaneous experiments in capitalist reform: the liberal New Deal in the United States, and the fascist, war-oriented Hitler dictatorship in Germany. The First Soviet Five-Year Plan, launched a few years earlier, suddenly began to appear to a crisis-ridden world as a beacon of hope, a possible way out for humanity afflicted with the peculiarly modern plague of poverty in the midst of plenty.

Nothing I had learned in the course of what was presumably the best education available in the United States had prepared me to expect, and still less to understand, any of these momentous developments. My state of mind as I arrived in London in the fall of 1932 was one of bewilderment and confusion edged with resentment at the irrelevance of what I had spent the last four years trying to learn. Whether I knew it or not I was a perfect candidate for conversion to new ways of thinking. And fortunately for me the situation at the London School was very favorable. The brand of economics in vogue, a sort of Austrian-Swedish mixture, was distinctive but basically a variant of the bourgeois orthodoxy I had grown up with. But there was Harold Laski in political science, a brilliant teacher who had been fired from Harvard for his role in the Boston police strike of 1919, entering the most radical phase of a colorful career and exposing a wide circle of students to a sympathetic interpretation of Marxian ideas. And above all there were the graduate students in all the social sciences, a variegated group from all over the world (the British Empire was still intact), who, unlike any students I had known in the United States, were in a continuous state of intellectual and political ferment. It was in this stimulating atmosphere, and mostly through fellow students, that I first came into contact with Marxism and what were then its major representatives in the West: left social democrats, orthodox Communists, and Trotskyists. At that stage the differences among them interested me very little; what was of enormous importance was that I soon began to see the world through different eyes. What up to then had seemed a senseless chaos of inexplicable disasters now appeared as the logical, indeed the inevitable, consequence of the normal functioning of capitalism and imperialism. And I had as little difficulty as most of my new friends in accepting the thesis that the way out of the crisis was through revolution and socialism, a course that the Russian Bolsheviks were pioneering and in which they needed all the support like-minded people in the rest of the world could give them.

I returned to the United States after my year at the London School a convinced but very ignorant Marxist. By the fall of 1933, things were already different at home from the way they had been only a year earlier. The shocking growth of unemployment to a quarter of the labor force, the collapse of the banking system, and the beginnings of New Deal reforms—not to mention developments abroad—had unleashed powerful social movements that had their reflection in intellectual and academic circles. Graduate students and younger faculty members at some of the larger universities like Harvard began to take an active interest in Marxism: discussion groups proliferated, and even a few, formal course offerings made their appearance.

It was under these circumstances that I acquired a mission in life, not all at once and self-consciously but gradually and through a practice that had a logic of its own. That mission was to do what I could to make Marxism an integral and respected part of the intellectual life of the country, or, put in other terms, to take part in establishing a serious and authentic North American brand of Marxism. (I say North American not because it is an altogether accurate characterization but because it corresponds to the practice of our friends and colleagues in Latin America who quite rightly object to the implied arrogance of any nation in the Western Hemisphere describing itself as American without qualification.)

Adopting this course involved learning and teaching, writing, and finally editing and publishing. For the remainder of the 1930s and up to 1942 I had the advantages of working in an academic environment, but that became very difficult after World War II. The upsurge of U.S. imperialism on a global scale was matched by a powerful wave of reaction internally, and for nearly two decades U.S. colleges and universities were virtually closed to Marxists and Marxism. In economics the only significant exception was the late

Paul Baran, who had been granted tenure at Stanford before the witch-hunting mania known as McCarthyism swept the country, turning its institutions of higher learning into accomplices in the suppression of radical thought. It was not until the birth of powerful new movements of protest in the 1960s—the civil rights movement and the anti-Vietnam war movement—that a renaissance of radical thought became possible and the colleges and universities could muster up the courage to support, at least here and there and in small ways, the ideals of academic freedom and unfettered discussion, which they had inherited from the founding fathers of the Republic and to which they had never ceased to pay lip service.

During this difficult period, Marxism, to the extent that it was tolerated at all, obviously had to live on the margins of U.S. society with no institutional base and no financial support from even the most liberal of private foundations. Recognizing this, the late Leo Huberman and I founded *Monthly Review* (subtitled "An Independent Socialist Magazine") with a few thousand dollars contributed by personal friends and an initial circulation of 400 subscribers. The first issue appeared in May 1949, which means that *Monthly Review* is now (1981) in its thirty-third year of publication. Two years later we began publishing books under the imprint of Monthly Review Press, at first simply as a means of assuring publication for books written by well-known authors like I. F. Stone and Harvey O'Connor who, in the repressive political atmosphere of the time, were being effectively boycotted by established publishing houses. Later on we expanded MR Press beyond this original function to become what I think is now generally recognized to be the leading publisher of Marxist and radical books in the English language. The magazine also expanded not only in terms of the number of subscribers but also through the establishment of several foreign-language editions: at the present time it is published in Italian in Rome, in Spanish in Barcelona, and in Greek in Athens.

In speaking of *Monthly Review* I have used the word "we." Originally that referred to Leo Huberman and myself, but in the course of time a number of other distinguished Marxist writers became closely associated with the enterprise. One was Paul Baran, whose book *The Political Economy of Growth,* published by MR Press in 1957, played a key role in advancing and deepening Marxist ideas on development and underdevelopment and their mutual interaction. Another was Harry Braverman, who became director of MR Press in 1967 and whose book *Labor and Monopoly Capital*, published by MR Press in 1974, has performed a similar role with respect to Marxist ideas on the labor process and the composition of the working class in advanced capitalist societies. And a third was Harry Magdoff, who became co-editor of *Monthly Review* after Leo Huberman's death in 1968 and whose book *The Age of Imperialism*, published by MR Press in 1969, is widely considered to be the standard Marxist work on U.S. imperialism in the post-World War II period.

One occasionally encounters references to a *Monthly Review* school of Marxism. If this is interpreted to mean, as I think the term "school" often is, a body of ideas inspired and guided by one or two dominant personalities, it is definitely misleading. Each member of the group that has been closely associated with MR came to Marxism by a different route and under a different combination of influences. The topics they chose to work on and the emphases they developed grew out of their own experiences and interests. If, on the other hand, "school" is taken to mean no more than that the members of the group have cooperated harmoniously, have criticized and influenced each other's ideas, and have produced a flow of work that is generally internally consistent and has helped to shape a tendency within the overall framework of Marxism that has appealed to and in turn been further developed by younger radical intellectuals and political activists not only in North America but also in other regions, both developed and underdeveloped, of the capitalist world—if this is what is meant by "school" then I have no objection and indeed can only hope that the implied characterization of MR's role and performance is deserved. But there is a corollary that I would ask you to bear in mind. The fact that an MR school exists only in the rather special sense I have indicated means that it has no authoritative representatives or spokespeople. Certainly the contents of these lectures have been greatly, and in some respects decisively, shaped by my having been privileged to work with my colleagues at MR, but I do not presume to speak for them any more than any of them would ever have presumed to speak for me.

The period about which I have been speaking, the nearly half century from the early 1930s to the end of the 1970s, was of course one of the most eventful in human history. It was a period of tremendous upheavals and profound changes on a world scale. And ways of interpreting the world as well as efforts to guide change in desirable directions have been caught up in the swift flow of events. Marxism—considered, as it should be, as an enterprise in both interpretation and guidance of change—has been particularly strongly affected. On the one hand, it has expanded enormously in terms of both its political influence and the numbers of its adherents, while on the other hand, its internal divisions and conflicts have multiplied and proliferated. In what follows I do not want to try to describe this process or analyze the stage at which it has now arrived—formidable and in any case probably not very rewarding tasks—but rather to bring together and present as intelligibly as I can the gist of my own thoughts on certain aspects of the present state of Marxism and some of the themes which occupy a central place in the Marxist universe of discourse.

First of all, I need a frame of reference not only as a point of departure but as a set of guidelines to be used in interpreting and criticizing a variety of ideas, theories, and formulations. For me this starting point can only be what Marx and Engels called the dialectical mode of thought, as contrasted to the metaphysical mode of thought which, paradoxical though it may seem, had been brought to its highest level of development by the methods and successes of modern science. But before we get to that, a few words must be said about what I understand to be the Marxist meaning of materialism.

For Marx and Engels materialism, as even a cursory reading of the first hundred pages of their joint work *The German Ideology* should make clear, is simply the obverse and alternative to idealism. It holds that ideas do not have an independent or primary existence; that they emanate from humanity and society; and that humanity and society are integral parts of a nature that existed before there was (terrestrial) life, including human life, and will continue to exist after it has become extinct. Dualities such as matter vs. spirit or mind vs. body are thus pseudo-problems; the infinite variety of nature is a manifestation of different modes and levels of organization of the ultimate building blocks of the universe (if indeed there are any such ultimate building blocks, a question about which the best scientists nowadays seem to be very unclear but the answer to which, if one were to be forthcoming, would in no way affect the validity or relevance of the Marxist conception of materialism). There is thus no unbridgeable divide between nature and society, nor, as a consequence, between natural and social sciences. Every science has as its object to understand/explain some aspect of reality; but since all aspects of reality have special problems and characteristics, it follows that each science has at least in some measure to devise its own methods and procedures, and that the ease and extent to which reliable knowledge can be attained vary widely from one to another. This, however, is no reason for reserving the term "science" for the more successful ones and denying it to those with less tractable subject matters.

With so much by way of introduction we can go on to consider the dialectical mode of thought. And here I want to introduce two quotations, one lengthy and one brief, from Engels' *Anti-Dühring*, in my opinion a masterpiece of exposition and clarification that has too often been neglected or put down precisely because it was addressed to a popular audience rather than to an elite of self-anointed experts. The first quotation occurs in the first chapter of Part I, entitled "General":

> When we reflect on nature, or the history of mankind, or our own intellectual activity, the first picture presented to us is of an endless maze of relations and interactions, in which nothing remains what, where, and as it was, but everything moves, changes, comes into being and passes out of existence. This primitive, naive, yet intrinsically correct conception of the world was that of ancient Greek philosophy, and was first clearly formulated by Heraclitus: everything is and also is not, for everything is in *flux*, is constantly changing, constantly coming into being and passing away. But this conception, correctly as it covers the general character of the picture of phenomena as a whole, is yet inadequate to explain the details of which this total picture is composed; and so long as we do not understand these, we also have no clear idea of the picture as a whole. In order to understand these details, we must detach them from their natural

or historical connections and examine each one separately as to its nature, its special causes and effects, etc. This is primarily the task of natural science and historical research—branches of science which the Greeks of the classical period, on very good grounds, relegated to a merely subordinate position, because they had first of all to collect materials for these sciences to work upon. The beginnings of the exact investigation of nature were first developed by the Greeks of the Alexandrian period, and later on in the Middle Ages were further developed by the Arabs. Real natural science, however, dates only from the second half of the fifteenth century, and from then on it has advanced with constantly increasing rapidity.

The analysis of nature into its individual parts, the grouping of the different natural processes and natural objects in definite classes, the study of the internal anatomy of organic bodies in their manifold forms—these were the fundamental conditions of the gigantic strides in our knowledge of nature which have been made during the last four hundred years. But this method of investigation has also left us as a legacy the habit of observing natural objects and natural processes in their isolation, detached from the whole vast interconnection of things; and therefore not in their motion, but in their repose; not in their life, but in their death. And when, as with the case of Bacon and Locke, this way of looking at things was transferred from natural science to philosophy, it produced the specific narrow-mindedness of the last centuries, the metaphysical mode of thought.

To the metaphysician, things and their mental images, ideas, are isolated, to be considered one after the other apart from each other, rigid, fixed objects of investigation given once for all. He thinks in absolutely discontinuous antitheses.... For him a thing either exists, or it does not exist; it is equally impossible for a thing to be itself and at the same time something else. Positive and negative absolutely exclude one another; cause and effect stand in equally rigid antithesis one to the other. At first sight this mode of thought seems to us extremely plausible because it is the mode of thought of common sense. But sound common sense, respectable fellow as he is within the homely precincts of his own four walls, has most wonderful adventures as soon as he ventures out into the wide world of scientific research. Here the metaphysical mode of outlook, justifiable and even necessary as it is in domains whose extent varies according to the nature of the object under investigation, nevertheless sooner or later always reaches a limit beyond which it becomes one-sided, limited, abstract, and loses its way in insoluble contradictions.

And this is so because in considering individual things it loses sight of their connections; in contemplating their existence it forgets their coming into being and passing away; in looking at them at rest it leaves their motion out of account; because it cannot see the woods for the trees. (New York: International Publishers, n.d., pp. 27–28)

The second quotation from *Anti-Dühring* comes from the Preface to the 1885 edition (seven years after the work was first published in book form):

> It is ... the polar antagonisms put forward as irreconcilable and insoluble, the forcibly fixed lines of demarcation and distinctions between classes, which have given modern theoretical natural science its restricted and metaphysical character. The recognition that these antagonisms and distinctions are in fact to be found in nature, but only with relative validity, and that on the other hand their imagined rigidity and absoluteness have been introduced into nature only by our minds—this recognition is the kernel of the dialectical conception of nature. (Ibid., p. 19)

I have included these passages from Engels rather than simply recommending that you read and study them for two reasons: first, because I believe that they constitute the clearest and at the same time perhaps the most neglected statement by either Marx or Engels of their basic way of thinking and apprehending the world; and second, because I am distressed by the extent to which the metaphysical mode of thought, the nature and limitations of which Engels so clearly exposes, has invaded present-day Marxism. If this invasion is to be effectively combated, as I am convinced it must be, this can be done not by criticizing one or another of its manifestations but by tracing it back to its root in a neglect or perversion of the fundamental tenets of Marxism.

Let me illustrate by what I think it is hardly an exaggeration to call the fetishization of the "mode of production" concept in a large and growing body of Marxist writing. I have no objection to the concept as such; in fact I think it can often be useful when carefully used as a tool of historical research. This involves, in Engels' language, recognizing that the "distinctions" on which the concept is based are indeed "to be found in nature," of which we recall society and history are integral parts, but "only with relative validity," which in this case can be interpreted to mean with a great deal of validity in some times and places, with less in others, and perhaps none at all in still others. These are matters that can be established not by appeal to the concept itself but by actual investigation and analysis.

But what we are too often offered these days is a view of history consisting of a sort of smorgasbord of modes of production, variously combined and arranged to be sure, but without any recognition—again in the words of Engels—that "their imagined rigidity and absoluteness have been introduced into nature by our minds." And to what extremes these qualities of rigidity and absoluteness are sometimes carried!

Modes of production, it seems, all have the same structure and the same relation to society as a whole. They consist of two interacting parts, the forces of production and the relations of production, which together constitute the base or foundation on which rests a superstructure of government, laws, religion, culture and arts, education and ideas, in short, everything that isn't already included in the base. Modes of production of course are not static structures, but neither do they change in arbitrary or random ways. Fortunately for those who seek to understand what happens in history, they all operate in much the same way. When a mode of production is functioning normally, there is a correspondence between the forces and relations of production in the sense that the relations foster the development of the forces. But in the course of time the forces outgrow the relations that become fetters rather than aids to further development. This ushers in a period of revolution that transforms the relations of production and with them the mode of production itself. With the new base the superstructure is likewise more or less rapidly transformed, and the whole cycle begins again.

Here we have what appears to be a universally valid schema for understanding history. The genesis, direction, and modalities of change are mapped out, and the appropriate points for human intervention to hasten and smooth the process, different for different stages in the development of a given mode of production, are more or less clearly indicated. It is no wonder that this way of thinking has exercised such a fascination for generations of Marxists, and that now, in a time that nearly everyone considers to be a revolutionary epoch *par excellence*, it should steadily attract new converts.

And yet we have to ask whether it is really a Marxist way of thinking. It has its origin in the writings of Marx and Engels in one place and one place only, the brief Preface to Marx's *Critique of Political Economy* (1859). The purpose of this Preface was not to expound a scientific theory but to give readers information that would help them to understand the book and the point of view from which it was written. Most of this information was autobiographical, leading up to an explanation of how the author came to focus his research on political economy, the subject matter of the book. This in turn gave rise to a "general conclusion" which "once reached ... served as the guiding thread in my studies." There then follows an exposition, couched in very general terms, of the schema sketched above—forces and relations of production, base and superstructure, revolutionary transformations. The "general conclusion" then ends with speculations on two themes that were doubtless closely connected in Marx's mind but for which subsequent history has provided little support: (1) "A social system," Marx stated, "never perishes before all the productive forces have developed for which it is wide enough; and new, higher productive relations never come into being before the material conditions have been brought to maturity within the womb of the old society." And (2) "In broad outline, the Asiatic, the ancient, the feudal, and the modern bourgeois modes of production can be indicated as progressive epochs in the economic system of society. Bourgeois productive relationships are the last antagonistic form of the social process of production . . . : but the productive forces developing within the womb of bourgeois society at the same time create the material conditions for the solution of this antagonism. With this social system, therefore, the pre-history of human society comes to a close."

If one examines this Preface as a whole and in context, rather than simply lifting out a few statements that are formulated in general terms, it is unmistakably clear that what Marx was talking about was capitalism, not history in general. Political economy, of course, meant the political economy of capitalism: Marx always used the term in this sense; it was therefore the study of capitalism and not of any other forms of society that led to his "general conclusion"; the forces of production/relations of production and base/superstructure schema was evidently derived from his study of capitalism, including its origins, its development, and its presumed future; the revolution transforming relations of production that had become incompatible with growing forces of production undoubtedly referred to both the bourgeois revolution and to what Marx was certain was the coming proletarian revolution. The insertion of a single sentence listing Asiatic, ancient, feudal, and modern bourgeois modes of production as "progressive epochs in the economic system of society" does not contradict this interpretation: it was simply meant to emphasize the status of capitalism as one, and in Marx's view the last, in a long line of "antagonistic" forms of society. That he had no thought of reading back into those earlier societies the structure and mode of functioning characteristic of capitalism is conclusively proved by the well-known fact that it was precisely during the 1850s, when the *Critique of Political Economy* was taking shape, that Marx came to adopt the (erroneous) view of Asian society, in the words of the Indian Marxist historian Bipan Chandra, as "a stagnant changeless society which was incapable of change from within." Such a view obviously could not have been held simultaneously with a belief in the universal applicability of the schema set forth in the Preface to the *Critique*. Nor did Marx or Engels on any other occasion elaborate on the schema or seek to apply it to the understanding of precapitalist societies. This was the work of later Marxists, undertaken for their own reasons and purposes and not because it was a logical outgrowth of the Marxist interpretation of history.

We shall return to this theme later on when we come to the question of postcapitalist societies. In the meantime I want only to add, in order to avoid possible misunderstanding, that I believe that *as applied to capitalism* the schema of the Preface can yield useful insights and understanding. The reason is that under capitalism, unlike other forms of society, separating base from superstructure and locating the prime source of change in the base correspond to a deep-seated and palpable reality, namely, the unplanned and uncontrolled character of a predominantly commodity-producing economy. Furthermore, the distinction between forces of production (means of production, technology, and workers) and relations of production (the absolute dominance of capital over the production process, guaranteed by the system of private property) is there for everyone to see. And it does not take a profound knowledge of economic history to understand that underlying the great changes that have characterized the capitalist epoch has been a series of technological revolutions. Nor would anyone want to deny that these changes originating in the economy have more or less rapidly spread to other areas, including government and laws, philosophy and religion, culture and the arts, in short everything that is usually thought of as constituting the superstructure.

The schema of the Preface is thus by no means arbitrary or artificial as applied to the case of capitalism, from which, after all, it was originally derived. But it seems to me a great mistake to treat this schema as embodying "laws" of historical materialism that are universally valid. The essence of historical materialism is simply that every society has to produce what it consumes, and it has to consume in order to reproduce itself, to survive, and to carry on the myriad activities that together define it as a recognizable historical entity. Production is therefore fundamental in a universal and unique sense, and a scientific approach to the understanding of history has to take this as its starting point. Furthermore, it is obvious that the possibilities of production at any given time and place establish narrow, though certainly not rigidly defined, limits and constraints on what a particular society can actually accomplish.*

But when it comes to the processes of change that are always going on in every society (or mode of production if you prefer), even if at times they are so slow as to be practically invisible, there is no a priori reason to assume that they must have their origin or derive their impetus from the realm of production, as prescribed

---

*This seems to me to be the rational kernel of the concept of "determination in the last instance" to which some Marxists—notably the French philosopher Louis Althusser and his followers—have assigned a privileged position in their version of historical materialism. In my view, however, the determination which is said to prevail in the last instance is of a largely negative kind and hence of little value in explaining what happens as distinct from what does not happen. The danger is that in the hands of uncritical practitioners "determinism in the last instance" tends to become a mere formula, a pseudo-explanation that closes off rather than opening up the way to a serious analysis.

by the schema of the Preface. As Marx and Engels wrote in *The German Ideology:*

> The fact is ... that definite individuals who are productively active in a definite way enter into ... definite social and political relations. *Empirical observation must in each separate instance bring out empirically, and without any mystification and speculation, the connection of the social and political structure with production.* (3rd revised ed. [Moscow: Progress Publishers, 1976], p. 41, emphasis added)

My attention was called to this striking formulation by the recent book *Socialist Construction and Marxist Theory,* by Philip Corrigan, Harvie Ramsay, and Derek Sayer. The authors go on to draw the appropriate conclusion:

> On this premise, Marxism could sustain *no* general theory of the "connection of the social and political structure with production" comparable to the classical base/superstructure conception. For any such theory must involve either *a priori* or inductive generalization, and Marx rules out the first when he requires that we ascertain this connection "empirically," and the second when he enjoins us to do so for "each separate instance." (New York: Monthly Review Press, 1978, p. 6)

There is, of course, no contradiction between this view and the schema of the Preface if we interpret the latter, as I have done here, not as a statement of a general law of history but as a shorthand summary of findings *empirically* derived from a study of the *separate instance* of capitalism. Like all shorthand summaries, it is naturally oversimplified: it provides a useful framework for further study of capitalism but by no means a rigid or infallible formula. That this is the way Marx and Engels themselves understood the matter is amply demonstrated by their own historical writings that show few if any traces of base/superstructure orthodoxy.

Engels' famous letters to younger German followers in the years after Marx's death (Conrad Schmidt, Bloch, Mehring, Starkenburg) should be interpreted in the same sense. These were mostly written in response to questions about the role of the economic factor in historical materialism, questions that reflected a strong tendency, which still exists today, to turn historical materialism into a form of economic determinism. Engels argued against this tendency, without denying, however, that there was some ground for it:

Marx and I are ourselves partly to blame for the fact that younger writers sometimes lay more stress on the economic side than is due it. We had to emphasize this main principle in opposition to our adversaries who denied it, and we had not always the time, the place, or the opportunity to allow the other elements involved in the interaction to come into their rights. But when it was a case of presenting a section of history, that is, of a practical application, the thing was different and there no error was possible. (Engels to Bloch, September 21, 1890)

It is true that some of Engels' formulations in these letters suggest that the noneconomic elements in the "interaction" affect the form and timing rather than the substance of change and in this way give support to a doctrine of "determination in the last instance" that is pretty close to an economic determinism. But it is also possible to consider these formulations as an indication that Engels himself had not completely overcome the tendency to overstress the economic factor mentioned in the passage cited above from the letter to Bloch. Once the principle of interaction has been admitted, it is no longer possible to salvage a general law of the determination of noneconomic elements by economic (or superstructure by base). The problem becomes the one Marx and Engels had already identified in *The German Ideology*, i.e., the "empirical observation ... in each separate instance ... [of] the connection of the social and political structure with production." This does not rule out generalizations for which an empirical basis can be established, but it does most certainly rule out universally valid laws of history.

[2]
THE CONTRADICTIONS OF CAPITALISM

In this lecture I am going to focus entirely on capitalism, and I want to say right away that in this area it seems to me Marxist theory has made important forward strides in recent years. These advances have of course not been evenly assimilated, and it may even be true that an appreciation of their scope and importance has hardly penetrated to what may be called the textbook level, where what is taught seems generally to be a more or less adequate summary of selected parts of Marx's *Capital*. Not that this is necessarily bad: a good case could be made that the best introduction to Marxism will always be *Capital* itself. But capitalism has greatly changed and expanded in the last hundred years, and its analysis requires that the theory expounded by Marx should be supplemented and to some degree modified to take account of these developments as well as of the vastly increased amounts of knowledge that a century of accumulated research has provided. My purpose in this lecture and the one to follow is to try to sketch, in desperate brevity as Schumpeter used to say, the main outlines of an overall Marxist theory of capitalism in the last quarter of the twentieth century.

A commodity is something—a good or a service—produced for sale, not for use. All societies since the most primitive have been characterized by some commodity production, but only under capitalism has it become the dominant type of production; and only under capitalism has labor power, the capacity of the worker to perform useful labor, become a commodity, not exceptionally but in general. Workers, however, would not sell their capacity to perform useful labor to others if they possessed the means and materials of production necessary to produce goods and services for their own account, i.e., either for direct consumption or for sale on the market. It follows that the very existence of capitalism implies that a tremendous and indeed traumatic upheaval has already taken place in the structure of social relations. Producers, especially peasants, have been uprooted and separated from their traditional means of producing and acquiring a livelihood, with the result that they are obliged to sell their labor power in order to keep alive and reproduce their kind. And, for this to be possible, there must be another class of people in existence who possess means of production and enough money or capital to buy labor power and materials that can be combined in a process of producing commodities for sale on the market. Capitalism, therefore, comes into the world in the wake of two great and more or less contemporaneous historical processes—the formation of a propertyless working class on the one hand and of a property-owning capitalist class on the other (the former's lack of property as well as the latter's ownership of it presuppose and necessitate a coercive state that is, therefore, as essential to the existence of capitalism as the workers and capitalists themselves).

These twin processes of class formation are what Marx called "primitive accumulation." He described and analyzed it in its classical Western European setting, but this should not be allowed to obscure the fact that its occurrence there was by no means a unique historical experience: wherever and whenever capitalism has made its appearance on the face of the globe, it has been preceded and accompanied by a process of primitive accumulation, varying from case to case in significant respects but always identical in content. In an important sense this is the key to world history from the sixteenth century on.

No understanding of capitalism is possible without an understanding of capital. This is as true today as it was a hundred years ago and as true of capitalism on a local or regional scale as it is of capitalism on a national or global scale. Here Marx's exposition of the theory as presented in the first volume of *Capital* is as valid as ever and has never been surpassed. For present purposes we shall have to be content with the briefest possible summary.

We follow Marx in using a comparison between the circulation processes of simple commodity production (in which producers own their own means of production and satisfy their needs by exchanging products against those of other similarly situated producers) and capitalist production (in which the means of production are owned by capitalists). In simple commodity production, the producer goes to market with a commodity C, exchanges it for money M, and in turn buys other commodities C that are required for the satisfaction of producers' families' needs. Symbolically, this process can be represented by the formula C–M–C where the first C stands for a specific commodity being marketed by the producer, the M for the money the producer gets in exchange, and the second C for the bundle of useful commodities he buys with the money. Here we are obviously talking about a system of production for use, though the link is indirect: producers do not use their own products (or at least by no means all of them), but all the same their purpose in producing is to satisfy their needs, not to add to their wealth.

Matters are radically different when we come to capitalism, a society in which those who do the actual producing own no means of production, are unable to initiate and direct a process of production, and hence must sell their labor power to capitalists who do own means of production and therefore control the processes of production. Here the defining formula C–M–C must be replaced by its "opposite," M–C–M. What this symbolizes is that the capitalist who initiates the process of production starts with money M. With this, the capitalist purchases commodities C, consisting of means of production and labor power which are transformed through a process of production into finished commodities ready for sale. When the sale has been completed, the capitalist is left once again with money: the circuit is closed. This does not mean, however, that the C–M–C circuit is absent from or irrelevant to capitalism. Under capitalism the commodity labor power that the capitalist buys is not produced by capitalists but rather is produced within the working-class household and is possessed by the workers as a use value. But lacking means of production, they are unable to turn this use value into what they need in order to live and reproduce. They are therefore obliged to treat it as a commodity C that they sell to capitalists for money M, and with this in turn they buy other commodities C that possess for them a greater use value. This then is a C–M–C circuit formally identical to that which characterizes simple commodity production. The difference is that in simple commodity production the workers use their own labor power and means of production to produce commodities that they sell for money, while under capitalism they sell their labor power directly to capitalists for money.

Wherever the C–M–C circuit obtains, the first and last terms can be, and indeed normally are expected to be, quantitatively equal, i.e., to have the same exchange value. The rationale of the operation lies not in the realm of exchange value but in that of use value: for simple commodity producers, the C at the end has greater use value than the C at the beginning, and it is this increase in use value that motivates their behavior. Nothing of the sort exists in the M–C–M case. The first and last terms are both money, qualitatively homogeneous and lacking use value of its own. It follows that if the two M's are also quantitatively equal, the operation totally lacks a rationale: no capitalist is going to lay out money and organize a process of production in order to end up with the same amount of money possessed at the outset. We can therefore rewrite the formula as M–C–M' where $M' = M + \Delta M$. Here ΔM represents more money, or as Marx called it, surplus value (*Mehrwert*).

Before going any further we should ask where this surplus value comes from. Marx's answer—and here he was following a line of reasoning pioneered by the classical economists, especially David Ricardo—was that the value of labor power (which he identified with the value of the worker's means of subsistence) measured in hours of work is less than what the worker produces also measured in hours of work. Or, to put the point in other terms, that a part of the working day replaces the value of what the worker consumes, while the remainder of the working day produces surplus value. Thus if the working day is ten hours and it takes workers five hours to produce a value equivalent to their daily consumption, they will produce five hours' worth of surplus value for the capitalist. Marx called the first five hours "necessary labor" and the second five hours "surplus labor," and the ratio of surplus labor to necessary labor (in this case 100 percent) he called the "rate of exploitation" or, translated into value terms, the "rate of surplus value." Note that, other things remaining equal, if the length of the working day is increased, the worker produces more surplus value for the capitalist and the rate of surplus value is raised. Marx called this the production of "absolute surplus value." Conversely, and once again assuming everything else remains equal, if the productivity of workers is increased (through introduction of machinery, reorganization of the work process, speed-up) and the time required to produce their subsistence thereby reduced, the proportion of the working day devoted to necessary labor will fall and that devoted to surplus labor will rise. In this case too, the rate of surplus value will go up. Marx called this the production of "relative surplus value."

Let me digress for a moment to point out that these concepts (surplus value, rate of surplus value, absolute and relative surplus value), all derived from the basic underlying theory of labor value, provided Marx with the framework for viewing capitalism not as a static system of exchange relations, in the manner of neoclassical economic theory, but as a *historical process*. The early history of capitalism is seen not (or not only) as a chaos of rapine and violence but as the process through which the distinctive capitalist mode of production came into the world, with the capital/wage-labor relation replacing the lord/serf relation as the central relation of exploitation in a new form of class society. Every class society is characterized by the necessary/surplus labor dichotomy, hence by an implicit rate of exploitation, but only in capitalism does this take the value form, with the rate of exploitation expressing itself as a rate of surplus value. This, and *not* the rate of profit (as some Marxists nowadays seem to believe), is the crucial variable that enabled Marx to get a firm handle on the history of capitalism.

By dividing surplus value into two parts (absolute surplus value and relative surplus value, neither of which would make sense without the concept of a *rate* of surplus value), Marx was able to lay bare the anatomy of the class struggles that have been at the heart of the process of capitalist development from the beginning, and the very existence of which is ignored or denied by neoclassical economics. It was in Part 3 of the first volume of *Capital* dealing with absolute surplus value that he analyzed historic struggles over the length of the working day, which were still acute in his time in the advanced capitalist countries and have still to be fought out in many underdeveloped countries in our day as well. And in Part 4 dealing with relative surplus value he traced the evolution of the organization of the labor process and the introduction and improvement of machinery in what is surely the greatest tour de force in the entire literature of economic history.

I stress these points here for two reasons: First, because they are perfect illustrations of what I consider to be one of the most essential principles of Marxism, namely, that the purpose of theory is to guide the analysis of reality which, in the social sciences, means the analysis of history. And second, because they provide the decisive refutation of those, like Joan Robinson and Ian Steedman, who argue that value theory is in no way essential to the Marxian analysis of capitalism, and that the central concept should be not the rate of surplus value but the rate of profit.* To adopt this position, in my opinion, is to throw away the indispensable key to understanding the inner structure and history of capitalism.

Let us now return to the analysis of the capitalist circulation process symbolized by the formula M–C–M'. This refers to what happens in a given period of time, say a year: the capitalist lays out M at the beginning of the year and ends with M' at the close. But this is only the first step of an analysis: the capitalist does not shut down the business at the end of a single production cycle. The enterprise continues to operate from one cycle to the next into the indefinite future, often outliving generations of its capitalist owners. The capitalist who had a capital of M at the beginning of the first year starts the second with M', and this in turn becomes M'', M''', M'''', and so on in successive years. This is what Marx meant when he characterized capital as self-expanding value. Of course, not every unit of capital succeeds in living up to its ideal of endless expansion: many fall by the wayside or are swallowed

---

*The most explicit statement of this position is that of Steedman: "It can scarcely be overemphasized that the project of providing a materialist account of capitalist societies is dependent on Marx's value magnitude analysis *only* in the negative sense that continued adherence to the latter is a major fetter on the development of the former" (Ian Steedman, *Marx After Sraffa* [London: New Left Books, 1978]). This is the last sentence in the book and sums up the message to which the entire work is devoted.

up by luckier or more efficient rivals. But this only increases the unrelenting pressure to "try harder," and the harder they all try, the more marked becomes capitalism's essential nature as an expanding universe. Considered as a whole, capitalism *must* expand: the alternative is not a stable condition of zero growth, as some liberal reformists would like to believe, but convulsive contraction and deepening crisis.

So far we have assumed that the process of capitalist production and circulation proceeds smoothly through its various phases—that capitalists are able to purchase the kinds and quantities of labor power and means of production they need, that they encounter no hitches in the production process itself, and that they are able to sell their finished goods at their full value. None of these assumptions is necessarily fulfilled in practice. All are violated in varying degree and at different times. It is this fact that gives to the history of capitalism its extremely uneven and often crisis-ridden character. Let us pause briefly to look at some of the ways in which the circulation process can be interrupted or thrown out of kilter.

First, the availability of labor power and means of production. As far as the means of production are concerned, their supply is generally taken care of by the self-regulating mechanisms of the system itself (subsumed by Marx under the concept of the "law of value"), that is to say, capitalists will find it to their advantage to produce and sell at their value the means of production that other capitalists require. There are, however, exceptions, often very important ones. This is especially true when means of production like raw or semiprocessed materials must be acquired by the capitalists of one country from an area under a different political jurisdiction. Here the potential threat of disruption is always present and always provides a motive for the capitalists of the purchasing country, of course in conjunction with their state, to seek reliable control over the producing region. This, evidently, is one of the driving forces of imperialist expansion in the capitalist epoch.

When it comes to the supply of labor power, matters are more complicated. Labor power is not produced by capitalists in accordance with the dictates of the law of value, and there is no a priori reason to expect a rapid or effective adjustment of supply to demand.

Massive state intervention has therefore been the rule rather than the exception throughout the history of capitalism, ranging from measures designed to hasten the disintegration of precapitalist relations, through the importation of slave or indentured workers, to encouragement and subsidization of the immigration of free wage laborers (as in the case of the large-scale migrations of so-called guest workers in post-World War II Europe). Even a cursory look at the ethnic and racial composition of the Western Hemisphere, almost entirely a creation of the capitalist epoch, is enough to suggest the vast importance of these factors in modern global history.

Second, hitches in the production process. In considering absolute and relative surplus value, we have already noted that the production process itself is the locus of deep-seated conflicts between capital and labor. It needs only to be added that these conflicts frequently break out into open struggles in the form of strikes, lockouts, boycotts, and direct violence, with resulting disruptions in the production and circulation processes.

Finally, the sale of finished goods or, as Marx expressed it, the "realization" of the value produced in the process of production. Here the problem is not the ability of the individual capitalist to sell the product at value. In the normal course of events the capitalist will sometimes sell the product above value and sometimes below: that is the way the law of value works itself out. The problem is the ability of capitalists *in general* to sell their products at value. If they can, the circulation process operates smoothly; if they cannot, there is what the classical economists called a glut: production slows down, profits fall, unemployment increases, etc. As we know from long experience—and as Marx was one of the first to recognize—this happens frequently under capitalism, manifesting itself in more or less regular cycles as well as in longer periods of stagnation that usually overlap with cyclical declines.

Marx touched on these problems at many points in his economic writings, but he nowhere subjected them to a systematic analysis. It is, hence, not surprising that different interpretations of his theory, or what presumably would have been his theory had he lived to elaborate it, have been put forward by his followers. I will not attempt to review these various interpretations here, but instead will focus on aspects that I believe flow naturally from Marx's fundamental analysis of capital and, at the same time, provide the best basis for understanding the specific forms of capitalist crisis that are characteristic of our own period. I refer to what may appropriately be called an overaccumulation theory.

We already know that because of the nature of the system of which they form an integral part capitalists are accumulators: the question is why and in what sense they are also chronic *overaccumulators*. The answer of course is not that they are conscious or intentional overaccumulators but that in their inexorable drive to expand their capital, they act in ways that produce results none of them intended and, in fact, run counter to their best interests.

Here we must distinguish between two manifestations of overaccumulation, one of which is prolonged periods of stagnation, while the other is the regular business cycle that characteristically passes through successive phases of recovery, boom, crisis, recession, and again recovery. The first is always present as a tendency that, however, can be counteracted if the historical conjuncture is favorable; the second has operated continuously since at least the early years of the nineteenth century. Perhaps the clearest example of overlapping occurred in the 1930s, a decade of extraordinary stagnation with little or no growth in the U.S. Gross National Product (GNP) and unemployment rates ranging from 15 to 25 percent, but also embracing a full business cycle (crisis in 1929, recession to 1933, recovery from 1933 to 1937, and renewed recession in 1938 and 1939).

In what sense can it be said that the business cycle is a manifestation of overaccumulation? Assume that the economy is entering a recovery phase, emerging from a situation of slack demand for the products of both Department I (producing means of production) and Department II (producing consumption goods). Unemployment is high, profit and interest rates low, money and credit in ample supply. The impetus to recovery typically comes from the depletion of inventories in the preceding recession. When this reaches a certain point, capitalists find it necessary to begin rebuilding their inventories, which means hiring additional workers and expanding production in both Departments. Since there is a pool of unemployed to draw on, this can go on for some time without putting upward pressure on wages. As idle capacity is activated, overhead costs are spread over a growing number of units of production and profits move sharply upward.

Here is where overaccumulation enters the picture. Whenever a process of recovery from a relatively low level gets under way, there is always a theoretical possibility that capitalists could divide the increasing surplus value accruing to them between accumulation and raising their own consumption in such a way as to maintain a sustainable equilibrium between the expansion of Departments I and II. But this theoretical possibility is interesting only because it throws into sharp relief the fact that, under conditions of recovery, capitalists actually act in a quite different fashion. Their concern in the new, and from their point of view favorable, situation is to expand their individual capitals to the maximum attainable extent. This sets off an accumulation boom that is fueled by further increases in profits and by easily available credit. Demand for the output of Department II, however, grows more slowly than total production, which means that a disproportionate amount of investment is devoted to expanding Department I. Such a process can continue without interruption for a considerable period since, up to a point, the expansion of Department I creates the necessary demand for its own output. Sooner or later, however, an unsustainable disproportion between the growth of the two Departments emerges, and the accumulation boom begins to taper off. It is at this stage that additional contradictions develop, notably, rising wages and interest rates that at a certain stage reduce not only the rate of profit but also the total amount of profit. This disrupts the continuity of the accumulation process, precipitating the crisis, which in turn ushers in the recession phase of the cycle.

If we now express this reasoning in terms of the M–C–M' formula, we can say that capitalists are driven by their limitless hunger for more wealth, as well as by the pressures of competition, to expand the middle term that symbolizes the production of value and surplus value, without taking account or *being able to take account* of the consequences for the magnitude and composition of the final term that symbolizes the demand for finished products. That this line of reasoning is in accord with Marx's thinking is clearly shown by the following passage:

> The creation of ... surplus value is the object of the direct process of production. As soon as the available quantity of surplus value has been materialized in commodities, surplus value has been produced.... Now comes the second act of the process. The entire mass of commodities ... must be sold. If this is not done, or only partly accomplished, or only at prices which are below the prices of production [i.e., modified values], the laborer has been none the less exploited, but his exploitation does not realize as much for the capitalist. It may yield no surplus value at all for him, or it may even mean a partial or complete loss of his capital. The conditions of direct exploitation and those of the realization of surplus value are not identical. They are separated logically as well as by time and space. The first are only limited by the productive power of society, the last by the proportional relations of the various lines of production and by the consuming power of society. The last-named power is not determined either by the absolute productive power or by the absolute consuming power, but by the consuming power based on antagonistic conditions of distribution, which reduces the consumption of the great mass of the population to a variable minimum within more or less narrow limits. The consuming power is further restricted by the tendency to accumulate, the greed for an expansion of capital and a production of surplus value on an enlarged scale. (*Capital*, vol. III, Kerr ed., chap. 15, sect. 1, p. 286)

What is described here is, of course, a *tendency* to overaccumulation that is inherent in the very nature of capital. But whether and in what forms this tendency is translated into reality depends on what kind of countertendencies exist, and this is more a matter of the historical context within which the accumulation process unfolds than of the logic of the process as such. Here I think it is essential to make a distinction between the stages into which the history of capitalism can be divided.

There is fairly general agreement among Marxists (though by no means complete consensus) that the history of capitalism to date comprises three stages, with labels varying according to the angle of vision of the observer. The first is the mercantile stage, beginning in the sixteenth century and running through the eighteenth. From the point of view of the labor process and the organization of production, this was called by Marx the period of manufacture (handicraft production organized in factories and characterized by increasingly elaborate division of labor as described by Adam Smith in *The Wealth of Nations*). Department I (producing means of production) remained small throughout, both absolutely and relatively. Accumulation took place mainly in commerce, agriculture, and mining.

The second stage was inaugurated by the industrial revolution, beginning in the textile sector in the eighteenth century and spreading to industry generally during the nineteenth, which saw the flowering of what Marx called "modern industry" (*machino*facture as opposed to *manu*facture). Looked at from other angles, this has also been called the period of competitive capitalism or liberalism. The focus of accumulation shifted sharply toward industry, and particularly to the build-up of Department I, including not only factories but also a vast infrastructure of transportation and communications (turnpikes, canals, ports, steamships, railroads, telegraphs).

The third stage, usually labeled monopoly capitalism, begins toward the end of the nineteenth century with the concentration and centralization of capital and the accompanying spread of the corporate form of business organization. The economic structure characteristic of this stage is "mature" in the sense that both Departments are now well developed and capable of rapid expansion and adaptation to changes in markets, methods of production, and other types of innovation.

A further relevant aspect of the history of capitalism has to do with geographical expansion. First taking root in Western Europe, capitalism spread in its mercantile form to most areas of the globe during its first three centuries. But because long-distance transportation and communication were then mostly by sea, this type of expansion affected predominantly coastal and island regions. The real penetration of non-European continents takes place only in the nineteenth century with the development of railroads, the case of North America being only the most striking example.

The point I want to emphasize by this impressionistic overview of the history of capitalism is that the second stage, encompassing most of the nineteenth century, was uniquely favorable for the accumulation process.* The reason is that it was during this stage that Department I, starting virtually from scratch, grew to be a major part of the total economy. Department II of course also grew, by reason of expanding employment, rising real wages, and increasing per capita incomes of farmers and others outside the capital-labor circuit. But, on the average, the growth of Department II was slower than that of Department I, which means that over the period as a whole a large part of the demand for the output of Department I came from that Department itself: means of production, in other words, had to be devoted not only to replacing worn-out means of production and increasing the capacity to produce means of consumption, but also to increasing the capacity to produce more means of production. This is a process that is characteristic not of capitalism as such but of capitalism in a certain stage of development, maturing capitalism. There comes a time, sooner or later, when Department I is sufficiently built up to supply all the needs of replacing worn-out means of production, and, in addition, to provide the inputs for an ample expansion of Department II (the scope of which can and should be broadened to include governments as consumers of both civilian and military products, relatively unimportant in the nineteenth century but looming ever larger in our time).**

As long as Department I is experiencing long-term growth more rapidly than that of Department II, i.e., during the maturing process, a sharp spurt in the growth rate of Department I of the kind that occurs in the boom phase of the business cycle need not

---

*It was also the period which encompassed Marx's lifetime (1818–1883) and played a crucial role in shaping his thought. We shall return to this aspect in an appendix to this chapter on the law of the falling tendency of the rate of profit.

**This maturing process is of course not peculiar to capitalism but must be undergone by any society that, starting from a low level of economic development, wishes to industrialize. We can recognize it very clearly, though in an altered and even exaggerated form, in the development of the Soviet Union since the inauguration of the five-year plans in the late 1920s. All plans since then have given priority to the production of means of production, and it is only recently that there has been a shift in emphasis toward the production of consumption goods. It can be argued, I think correctly, that the Soviet Union went overboard in emulating the capitalist model and would have achieved better results by its own standards if it had slowed the planned rate of growth of its Department I.

cause a *lasting* disequilibrium in the proportion between the two Departments. During the downswing of the cycle the contraction is typically more severe in Department I than in Department II, and an appropriate proportionality between the two Departments can be more or less rapidly restored. But when the maturing process is over and the sustainable growth rate of Department I comes to depend essentially on its being geared to the growth of Department II, then matters are very different. If capitalists persist in trying to increase their capital (society's productive power) more rapidly than is warranted by society's consuming power (limited in the manner depicted by Marx in the quotation on p. 36 above), the result will be a build-up of excess capacity. As excess capacity grows, profit rates decline and the accumulation process slows down until a sustainable proportionality between the two Departments is again established. This will occur with the economy operating at substantially less than its full potential. In the absence of new stimuli (war, opening of new territories, significant technological or product innovations), this stagnant condition will persist: there is nothing in the logic of the reproduction process to push the economy off dead center and initiate a new period of expansion.

This does not mean that there are no ups and downs during a period of stagnation. In particular inventory fluctuations of the kind discussed above in connection with the causation of normal business cycles will continue to occur and to be reflected in overall expansions and contractions. This is at least part of the explanation of the swings during the stagnant 1930s, which were commented on above. At the same time, it must always be kept in mind that in interpreting concrete historical experiences many factors are at work that cannot be encompassed in a general theoretical analysis.

I have already stressed that capital, both individual units and as a whole, is self-expanding value. Overall, of course, the rate of expansion is limited by the amount of surplus value produced, realized, and available for accumulation. But this is not true of the individual units that can expand beyond this limit by absorbing or merging with other existing units. Expansion by internal accumulation Marx called "concentration of capital"; expansion by absorption or merger he called "centralization of capital." The two processes are complementary, working together to transform the economy from one of innumerable small competing units, as it still was when Marx wrote *Capital,* to one of giant monopolistic corporations, as it was beginning to be when Engels edited the manuscripts of the second and third volumes in the decade after Marx's death. Marx was the first economist to recognize and theorize this process that turned out to be so crucial in the succeeding century: he saw clearly its roots in the greater profitability of large units compared to small, on the one hand, and, on the other hand, in the capacity of the corporate form (then called the joint stock company) to assemble masses of capital for projects like railroads, which were far beyond the means of individual capitalists.

Marx thus made an excellent beginning in the analysis of monopoly capitalism, showing how and why it was the inevitable outgrowth of capitalism in its competitive stage. The first generation of his followers, particularly Hilferding and Lenin, built on this foundation. Hilferding, as the title of his major work (*Das Finanzkapital*) indicates, explored the financial aspects and stressed the relation between economic developments and trends in the political and cultural realms. Lenin connected the rule of monopoly-finance capital with the world-historical developments of the late nineteenth and early twentieth centuries that culminated in World War I and the Russian Revolution; and in so doing, he opened the door to a radical reconceptualization of the structure and functioning of capitalism as a global system comprising and pitting against each other a handful of highly developed imperialist nations and a much larger number of underdeveloped colonies, semicolonies, and dependencies. But then progress along these lines slowed down and, at least in the West (I cannot speak for Japan), came to a virtual halt. Part of the reason, I suspect, was the towering stature of Lenin who, for many Marxists of the period, was considered to have said the last word on all subjects he touched. Even more important was the pall of rigid orthodoxy that was a by-product of the Stalin era and that smothered or perverted scientific inquiry wherever it spread. In any case and whatever the reason, there was a long hiatus after Lenin; and it was only after World War II, in a fundamentally changed international situation and under the stimulus of a new wave of revolutionary activity in the weakest links of the imperialist chain, that the advance was resumed.

It would be interesting to analyze the course of the renaissance of creative Marxism in the post-World War II period, but obviously nothing as ambitious as that can be undertaken here. As far as monopoly capitalism is concerned, my immediate aim is simply to summarize what I take to be the main advances in one particular area, namely, the impact of growing concentration and centralization on the production, realization, and accumulation of surplus value. Other aspects having to do with the structure and functioning of capitalism as a global system will be the focus of attention in my next lecture.*

The normal functioning of the law of value presupposes competition among many units of capital, each too small in relation to the market in which it operates to have significant influence on the selling price. In these circumstances, the way to survive and expand is to turn out a better product at lower cost. Those capitalists who succeed enjoy an extra profit that, however, induces others to follow the same course (and/or attracts new capitalists into the industry). With lower average costs the value of the product declines, and as output increases price also falls toward a new equilibrium between value and price. Competition also works to equate price and value when, with average costs remaining the same, the demand for the product rises or falls, causing an increase in price and profit in the former case and a decrease in the latter. New capital is then attracted into the industry or marginal producers forced out until the new equilibrium has been reached. The point is that adjustments are effected through the mechanism of fluctuations of price (hence also of profit rates), which are caused not by the deliberate action of the producers but by changed conditions

---

*I use the term "monopoly capitalism" because it is widely used by Marxists and non-Marxists alike. The implication, however, is not that monopoly in the literal sense of one seller has replaced rivalry and struggle among a number of sellers, which is the everyday meaning of the term "competition." In this sense, competition not only continues to exist but is at least as fierce as it was in Marx's time. What have changed are the methods and consequences of competition. This subject is treated at greater length in Appendix B to this chapter.

of supply and demand. This reasoning in support of the theory of value was, of course, not original with Marx: it was part and parcel of classical political economy going back to Adam Smith and even earlier.*

At a certain point in the unfolding of the concentration/centralization process, the assumption that individual producers are too small to exercise a significant influence on the prices of their products loses its justification. When this happens in sectors of the economy that together dominate the functioning of the system as a whole, capitalism has passed from its competitive to its monopoly stage.

The widespread existence of monopoly, or, if you prefer, monopolistic competition, does not necessarily alter the total amounts of value and surplus value produced, but it does effect a redistribution of the surplus value in favor of the more monopolized industries and at the expense of the less monopolized, and, of course, even more at the expense of the sectors of the economy that remain competitive in the sense already explained. This means that as the monopolization process advances, more and more surplus value flows into the coffers of the biggest units of capital and less and less goes to the little ones. And since a larger unit of capital will be able to accumulate proportionately more than a smaller one, it follows that the greater the degree of monopoly, the greater will be the capacity of the economy to accumulate, and hence also to overaccumulate.

But this is not all. Monopoly not only enhances the capacity to accumulate; it also chokes off attractive outlets for capital investment. To put the point more concretely, the big monopolies tend to be very profitable and, therefore, able to accumulate rapidly, while at the same time they are afraid of spoiling their own market

---

*It will be noted that I speak here of values and not of what Marx called prices of production, which in his theory are not to be confused with market prices but are modified values. Prices of production play an important role in Marx's theory, but their relevance is not to the process of capital accumulation, the subject that concerns us here. It is important to note in this connection that Marx developed the whole framework of his theory of the production, realization, and accumulation of surplus value in the first volume of *Capital* without even mentioning prices of production.

by overinvesting. In addition, they set up whatever barriers they can to protect their monopolistic positions against outsiders invading their markets—for example, by maintaining a considerable margin of unused productive capacity that can be quickly activated in retaliation against unwanted newcomers.

Monopoly thus acts in two ways to intensify the contradictions of the accumulation process that, as we have already seen, are inherent in the M–C–M' formula: on the one hand, it raises the potential rate of accumulation, and, on the other hand, it restricts the profitable outlets into which the accumulated surplus value can flow. The result is to accentuate the tendency to overaccumulation. And this accentuation itself tends to increase over time whenever and wherever monopolization, especially through the progressive centralization of capital, is an ongoing process, as it has been since the beginning of the present century in Western Europe and the United States (and I believe also in Japan and indeed in most, if not all, other capitalist countries, underdeveloped as well as developed).

I want to conclude this all-too-brief discussion of the concentration and centralization of capital and the consequent transformation of competitive into monopoly capitalism with a few remarks which I believe, despite their speculative character, have a crucially important bearing on the present state of the world capitalist system and its probable development in the visible future.

Marx wrote that "the real barrier of capitalist production is capital itself." I have been arguing in effect that monopoly capital makes that barrier even bigger and more formidable. So much so that stagnation—a combination of sluggish growth, rising unemployment, and a chronically low level of utilization of productive capacity—has become *the normal condition of capitalist economies*. To the extent that this is not their actual state, the reason is not to be sought or found in the internal logic of the capitalist system, but in the infinitely more complex historical environment within which it operates and produces its effects. By the same token, the important unsolved, or only partly solved, theoretical problems of capitalism relate not so much to that internal logic, the framework for the analysis of which Marx himself so successfully elucidated, as to the interplay between it and the historical environment that sometimes unleashes capitalism's enormous expansionary potential and sometimes provides so little stimulation that the accumulation process grinds to a virtual standstill.

Whether this way of looking at capitalism in its monopoly stage is "correct" can be neither proved nor disproved. The interesting question is rather whether it provides a fruitful approach to the analysis of the history of the twentieth century. And here, I think, the answer is unambiguously in the affirmative. Focusing on the United States—both because I know it best and because it has been the leading capitalist country in recent times, playing the same role for us that Britain played for Marx in the nineteenth century—I would argue that there is really no other way to put the three great episodes of recent times into a consistent and meaningful perspective: the decade-long stagnation of the 1930s, the incredible upsurge of the World War II years, and the quarter century of relatively uninterrupted expansion from the late 1940s to the early 1970s, culminating in a relapse into what appears to be the beginnings of a new period of persistent stagnation.

I shall have more to say about this last period in my next lecture. In concluding this one, I want simply to call attention to the enormous, and I think too often neglected, significance of the wartime experience. The Gross National Product of the United States in real terms grew between 1940 and 1945 by some 75 percent at the very same time that 11 million men and women in the most productive age groups were being absorbed into the armed forces. Why? Because the barrier of capitalist production represented by capital itself was temporarily removed. It was not that some fantastic new productive potential was discovered or created: that was there all along. It was simply that an unrestricted market for capitalist production suddenly opened up and capitalists responded to it exactly as one would expect them to.

I believe that there is a lesson here that all of us, by which I mean humankind as a whole, are going to have to learn sooner or later. Marxists have always maintained that the productive forces generated by capitalism were powerful enough, if applied to the satisfaction of reasonable human needs, to eliminate poverty and create a society of abundance. A hundred years ago such claims were doubtless premature. But today in the developed capitalist countries they are based on demonstrable fact. The continuation of the rate of production achieved during World War II in the United States, of course with a suitable reorientation toward the fulfillment of needs rather than the proliferation of the means of destruction, would have sufficed in a historically short time to create for the people of the country a life of material abundance. And if a similar situation existed in the other advanced countries and the knowledge applied there were freely available to the presently underdeveloped countries, the whole world could be raised to a comparable level within a few generations. (I abstract from ecological considerations, but I am convinced that problems of this kind would be amenable to reasonable and even humanly advantageous solutions if production were genuinely directed to satisfying needs rather than maximizing profits.)

I conclude that what is perhaps the oldest dream of socialists and communists, that a decent life for all is within our reach, is now more solidly based than at any time in the past. Many disappointments and unhappy experiences, of course, have caused it to lose its once enormous appeal—at just the time, unfortunately, when it ought to be the other way around. Perhaps the time has come to revive the dream and again to dedicate ourselves to making it a reality.

[APPENDIX A]
THE LAW OF THE FALLING TENDENCY OF THE RATE OF PROFIT

Part 3 of the third volume of *Capital*, comprising some sixty pages, is devoted to what Marx called "The Law of the Falling Tendency of the Rate of Profit." Friedrich Engels, who prepared the volume for publication, wrote in his editor's Preface:

> Nothing was available for the third volume but a first draft, and it was very incomplete. The beginnings of the various sections were, as a rule, pretty carefully elaborated, or even polished as to style. But the farther one proceeded, the more sketchy and incomplete was the analysis, the more excursions it contained into side issues whose proper place in the argument was left for later decision, the longer and more complex became the sentences in which the rising thoughts were deposited as they came.

Given this background, one must naturally be cautious about the way one cites and interprets material from Volume 3. It contains many striking formulations and brilliant insights, but also ambiguities and inconsistencies. It must be read in the context of Marx's work as a whole and in accordance with one's understanding of his method and intentions. These are, inevitably, subjective matters about which views will differ, sometimes widely. The following brief comments should be read with this in mind.

But first it is necessary to dispose of certain clearly erroneous interpretations of the law. One confuses a falling *rate* of profit with a decline in the *amount* of profit (or surplus value) available for accumulation and concludes—logically once the premise is accepted—that Marx meant the law as an explanation of the eventual downfall of capitalism. But this is simply wrong. One could quote many passages, not only from the relevant Part 3 of Volume III, refuting this interpretation. Perhaps the most explicit is the following:

> We see ... that in spite of the progressive fall of the rate of profit, there may be an absolute increase of the number of laborers employed by capital, an absolute increase of the labor set in motion by it, an absolute increase of the mass of surplus labor absorbed, a resulting absolute increase of the produced surplus value, and consequently an absolute increase of the mass of the produced profit. And it *may* not only be so. On the basis of capitalist production, it *must* be so, aside from temporary fluctuations. (*Capital*, vol. III, Kerr ed., p. 255, emphasis in the original)

A second erroneous interpretation is to treat the law as a prediction. It should be obvious, however, that if this had been Marx's intention, he would have labeled it "the law of the falling rate of profit," leaving the word "tendency" out altogether. And he would not have followed the chapter entitled "The Theory of the Law" with another chapter of equal standing called "Counteracting Causes."

Finally, a third erroneous interpretation is that Marx intended the law as a theory, or at least as the basis of a theory, of crises and/or cycles. This is prima facie more plausible, since the long chapter entitled "Unraveling the Internal Contradictions of the Law," which follows the ones on the theory of the law and the counteracting causes, contains many highly interesting references to and partial analyses of various aspects of these most complex of all economic phenomena. But a close examination shows that the passages in question do not depend on the law as expounded in the previous two chapters, but rather relate to what are usually called problems of realization or to the vagaries of the credit system, all of which exist quite independently of any long-run tendencies of the profit rate. These are excellent examples of what Engels, in the above quotation from the preface to Volume III, called "excursions into side issues whose proper place in the argument was left for later decision."

Having disposed of these preliminaries, we can now proceed to what seem to me to be the two most interesting, and doubtless most controversial, questions relating to the law. (1) If it was not intended to explain either the eventual demise of capitalism or its periodic crises, why was Marx so fascinated by the law and why did he attach so much significance to it? And (2) why was he so convinced, as he undoubtedly was, that the foundations of the law were rooted in the essential nature of capitalist production? Let us consider these questions in turn.

The significance of the law. To understand why Marx considered the law so important, one must place the problem in the context of the time and, more specifically, of Marx's relation to classical political economy. The classical economists, led by Ricardo, had a similar law, only it was stated much more strongly than Marx's, i.e., not as a tendency but as an inevitable trend, and it gained for their teachings notoriety as the "dismal science." The reasoning was that economic expansion, propelled as in the case of Marx by capital accumulation, requires recourse to ever less fertile land. This sets in motion a process governed by diminishing returns and the Malthusian population law that leaves workers with unchanged real wages and divides the surplus (total output minus wages) increasingly in favor of landlords and to the disadvantage of capitalists. For a while profit might increase, but eventually it will be inexorably squeezed between wages and rent, with not only the total amount but also the rate of profit falling to the point where capitalists have no more incentive to accumulate. The end comes with the stationary state, most eloquently described by John Stuart Mill. The only way to put off the evil day would be to repeal the Corn Laws protecting English agriculture, in this way avoiding for a time the necessity of recourse to inferior lands. Ideologically and politically, classical political economy was thus the great weapon of the rising bourgeoisie in its struggle for free trade and dominance over the landed aristocracy.

Marx of course rejected all this, not, however, because of its logic but because of its premises. For him capital accumulation was not only a quantitative but also a qualitative process. It internalizes scientific and technological advances—in favor of capital and at the expense of labor—and thus repeals the law of diminishing returns (that, understood properly, is really not a law at all but a mere truism). And Marx contemptuously dismissed the Malthusian population theory as a "libel on the human race." He was thus able to conceive of capitalism not as a system that is winding down to an inevitable standstill, but as one with a fierce inner drive that has the historical mission of vastly multiplying the productive power of human labor. This does not mean, however, that it is a harmonious system with built-in controls and stabilizers: quite the contrary. It is a system laden with contradictions inherent to its nature that it can neither eliminate nor master. And Marx saw the law of the falling tendency of the rate of profit as a crucially important barometer of the intensity and ineluctability of these contradictions. The following passage, unnoticed in any discussion of the law with which I am familiar, eloquently sums up what I believe was, for Marx, the very heart of the matter:

> The rate of profit is the compelling power of capitalist production, and only such things are produced as yield a profit. Hence the fright of the English economists over the decline of the rate of profit. That the bare possibility of such a thing should worry Ricardo shows his profound understanding of the conditions of capitalist production. The reproach moved against him, that he has an eye only to the development of the productive forces regardless of "human beings," regardless of the sacrifices in human beings and capital *values* incurred, strikes precisely his strong point. The development of the productive forces of social labor is the historical task and privilege of capital. It is precisely in this way that it unconsciously creates the material requirements of a higher mode of production. What worries Ricardo is the fact that the rate of profit, the stimulating principle of capitalist production, the fundamental premise and driving force of accumulation, should be endangered by the development of production itself.... There is indeed something deeper than this hidden at this point, which he vaguely feels. It is here demonstrated in a purely economic way, that is, from a bourgeois point of view, within the confines of capitalist understanding, from the standpoint of capitalist production itself, that it has a barrier, that it is relative, that it is not an absolute but only a historical mode of production corresponding to a definite and limited epoch in the development of the material conditions of production. (Ibid., pp. 304–5)

The foundations of the law. To understand why Marx was convinced that the law was rooted in the nature of capitalist production, we need to recall his formulation of the law. In his theory the value of a commodity (w) is made up of the sum of constant capital (c), variable capital (v), and surplus value (s): $w = c + v + s$.* The rate of profit (p) is the ratio of surplus value to total capital, while the rate of surplus value (s') is the ratio of surplus value to variable capital. One further concept derived from the value formula figures in Marx's theory, the ratio of constant capital to variable capital, which he called the organic composition of capital (o). The interrelation of these concepts is shown as follows:

$$p = \frac{s}{c+v} = \frac{\frac{s}{v}}{\frac{c}{v}+\frac{v}{v}} = \frac{s'}{o+1}$$

From which it follows that the rate of profit varies directly with the rate of surplus value and inversely with the organic composition of capital. The law, therefore, can be restated, that in the course of capitalist development the organic composition of capital tends to rise relatively more rapidly than the rate of surplus value.

This, of course, is not a logical necessity. That both the rate of surplus value and the organic composition would increase over time was an assumption that Marx certainly thought was obvious and uncontroversial.** But why he should have made the additional assumption that the organic composition increases relatively more rapidly than the rate of surplus value is not at all obvious. Some Marxists have attempted to solve the problem by a kind of pseudo-mathematical line of reasoning. From a purely mathematical standpoint, the argument goes, there is no limit to the increase in the organic composition. If the ratio of constant to variable capital starts at one-to-one, it can obviously rise to two-to-one, ten-to-

---

*Constant capital consists of the value of material inputs, including wear and tear of machinery, which is transferred to the product; variable capital is the value of labor power paid to the worker in the form of wages; and surplus value is the product of surplus labor (see p. 29 above).

**In expounding the "theory of the law," Marx assumed a constant rate of surplus value and a rising organic composition. But this was clearly no more than a device for simplifying the presentation of the logic of the argument. The whole thrust of his analysis in all three volumes of *Capital* was that the accumulation process brings in its train a more intense exploitation of labor by capital, i.e., a rising rate of surplus value.

one, or whatever your imagination fancies. On the other hand there is a limit to the increase in the rate of surplus value: necessary labor can never be reduced to zero, since that would mean that workers would starve to death. From this the conclusion is drawn that the organic composition can rise indefinitely while the increase in the rate of surplus value runs into an impenetrable barrier. QED. The argument is silly, even from a mathematical standpoint. The amount of necessary labor can tend toward zero without ever reaching it (total automation with only one worker needed to set the apparatus in motion and watch over its functioning, all others living on unemployment insurance paid out of surplus value), which would mean that both the rate of surplus value and the organic composition (ratio of constant to variable capital) would tend toward infinity. Such science-fiction fantasies have their interest, but hardly in relation to the law of the falling tendency of the rate of profit. In the real world the range of variation of the organic composition is likely to be of the same order of magnitude as that of the rate of surplus value; and such statistical studies as have been attempted, while beset with conceptual difficulties and lack of appropriate data, have shown that this is indeed the case. If we are to understand why Marx thought the organic composition would rise relatively more rapidly than the rate of surplus value, we must look elsewhere, to the realm of history rather than hypothetical possibilities. The following passage, at the beginning of the chapter on "Counteracting Causes," holds the key:

> If we consider the enormous development of the productive powers of labor, even comparing but the last 30 years with all former periods; if we consider in particular the enormous mass of fixed capital, aside from machinery in the strict meaning of the term, passing into the process of social production as a whole, then the difficulty which has hitherto troubled the vulgar economists, namely, that of finding an explanation for the falling rate of profit, gives way to its opposite, namely, to the question: how is it that this fall is not greater and more rapid? There must be some counteracting influences at work which thwart and annul the effects of this general law, leaving to it merely the character of a tendency. (Ibid., p. 272)

This was written by one whose adult life coincided with the high tide of the industrial revolution. An economy that a century earlier had still been characterized by predominantly handicraft methods of production (manufacture in the literal sense), that was deep into the transition to what Marx called "modern industry,"* and that was well on its way to becoming a mature capitalism in the sense described above (p. 37). As pointed out there, Department I producing means of production grew in this period from rudimentary beginnings to become in important ways the decisive sector of the economy. And the counterpart of this, of course, was an enormous increase in the organic composition of the society's total capital. Under these circumstances it is no wonder that Marx thought the problem was not why the rate of profit should fall but why the fall was not steeper and more rapid.**

If the foregoing reasoning is accepted, it follows that Marx's law of the falling tendency of the rate of profit was rooted in the conditions of nineteenth-century capitalism. But it must be added that it loses plausibility when applied to the fully mature capitalism that emerged in the twentieth century. During the transition from *manu*facture to *machino*facture, increases in labor productivity could be assumed to involve, as a general rule, a rise in the organic composition of capital. It would also normally involve a rise in the rate of surplus value, but there is no reason to assume that the latter must outweigh the former; and as long as this is the case, it makes sense to talk of a *tendency* for the rate of profit to fall. But once industry has been comprehensively mechanized, the situation changes. The way for capitalists to increase labor productivity (and hence raise their rate of profit) can no longer be assumed generally to be through substituting machinery for living labor.

Capital, Volume I, Chapter 15 ("Machinery and Modern Industry"). The entire Part 4, entitled "Production of Relative Surplus Value," of which Chapter 15 constitutes more than two-thirds, should be considered and studied as an essential complement to Part 3 of the third volume dealing with the law of the falling tendency of the rate of profit. Where inconsistencies exist, as I believe they do, the text of Volume I should be accorded priority. It was written *after* the materials that went to make up Volume III; and, unlike the latter, Marx himself prepared it for the printer and saw it through to publication.

**Whether there was really a fall in the rate of profit during the period in question is impossible to say. There are no reliable data that would permit an answer.

It may equally well be through substituting more productive machines and processes for less productive machines and processes.* And there is no particular reason to assume that this must involve either an increase or a decrease in the organic composition of capital. Since, on the other hand, it *can* be assumed to involve an increase in the rate of surplus value, it would be reasonable in these circumstances to speak of a rising tendency of the rate of profit (always bearing in mind the existence of counteracting causes).

In concluding this brief discussion of Marx's law of the falling tendency of the rate of profit, it may be useful to note that such statistical evidence as is available indicates that the organic composition of capital rose in accordance with Marx's assumption through the nineteenth and into the twentieth century, but that since then the trend has been in the other direction. Most studies bearing on the issue have been carried out by bourgeois researchers, with a consequent problem of translating their findings into the language of Marxism. But at least one, that of Joseph Gilman, is the work of a Marxist economist, and its results are striking: the organic composition of capital in the United States rose up to 1919, leveled off in the 1920s, and thereafter declined (except for the early 1930s when the trend was obliterated by the severity of the Great Depression).** Gilman's statistical procedures have been criticized, but to my knowledge no one has claimed that his findings would have been basically different if all the criticisms had been

---

*Marx was well aware of this form of capitalist behavior, and he could have given it a more prominent place than he did in capitalism's "laws of motion." Cf. the following passage from Volume I, Chapter 24 ("Conversion of Surplus Value into Capital"):

> A part of the functioning constant capital consists of instruments of labor such as machinery, etc., which are not consumed, and therefore not reproduced or replaced by new ones of the same kind until after long periods of time.... If the productiveness of labor has, during the using up of these instruments of labor, increased (and it develops continually with the uninterrupted advance of science and technology), cheaper machines, tools, apparatus, etc., replace the old. The old capital is reproduced in a more productive form, apart from the constant detail improvements in the instruments of labor already in use. (*Capital*, vol. I, Kerr ed., p. 663)

**Joseph M. Gilman, *The Falling Rate of Profit* (New York: Cameron Associates, 1958). See especially the chart on p. 37 and the fold-out statistical table facing p. 61.

fully met. This, of course, does not imply that the organic composition of capital in the advanced capitalist countries is necessarily falling now or can only fall in the future. But I think it is fair to say that it does demonstrate the futility of theorizing which starts from the assumption of an ineluctably rising organic composition.

Reliable data on historical movements of the rate of profit do not exist. But even if they did, they would not throw any useful light on the validity or lack of validity of the Marxian law. The reason is that in practice changes in the rate of profit are determined not only by movements in the rate of surplus value and the organic composition of capital, but by many other factors as well. Marx himself included most of them in the chapter on "counteracting causes." But there are others that he did not discuss, notably the degree of monopoly in the economy as a whole and the kind of secular stagnation with which we have become familiar in the last half century. Some of these factors are related to the rate of profit as both cause and effect, a fact that would prevent the drawing of clear-cut inferences from much more precise and reliable data than we have at our disposal.

[APPENDIX B]
COMPETITION AND MONOPOLY

In his *Principles of Political Economy* John Stuart Mill summed up the classical view of competition as follows:

> Political economists ... are apt to express themselves as if they thought that competition actually does, in all cases, whatever it can be shown to be the tendency of competition to do. This is partly intelligible, if we consider that only through the principle of competition has political economy any pretension to the character of a science. So far as rents, profits, wages, prices, are determined by competition, laws may be assigned for them. Assume competition to be their exclusive regulator, and principles of broad generality and scientific precision may be laid down, according to which they will be regulated. The political economist justly deems this his proper business: and as an abstract or hypothetical science, political economy cannot be required to do, and indeed cannot do, anything more. (2 vols., vol. I, 5th ed. [New York: D. Appleton and Co., 1888], p. 301)

Competition, in other words, does not determine the *content* of the laws of economics, but it does provide the pressures that constrain economic subjects (capitalists, workers, landlords, consumers, etc.) to act in ways that conform to these laws. Marx's view was basically the same, though he expressed it differently. The following passages from the *Grundrisse* are representative of his comments on competition:

> Competition generally, this essential locomotive force of the bourgeois economy, does not establish its laws, but is rather their executor. Unlimited competition is therefore not the presupposition for the truth of the economic laws, but rather the consequence—the form of appearance in which their necessity realizes itself.... Com-

petition therefore does not *explain* these laws; rather, it lets them be *seen*, but does not produce them. (Martin Nicolaus, trans. [New York: Vintage, 1973], p. 552)

Competition executes the inner laws of capital; makes them into compulsory laws toward the individual capital, but it does not invent them. It realizes them. (p. 752)

Free competition is the relation of capital to itself as another capital, i.e., the real conduct of capital as capital. The inner laws of capital—which appear merely as tendencies in the preliminary historic stages of its development—are for the first time posited as laws; production founded on capital for the first time posits itself in the form adequate to it only insofar as and to the extent that free competition develops, for it is the free development of the mode of production founded on capital; the free development of its conditions and of itself as the process which constantly reproduces these conditions.... Free competition is the real development of capital. By its means what corresponds to the nature of capital is posited as external necessity for the individual capital; what corresponds to the concept of capital is posited as external necessity for the mode of production founded on capital. The reciprocal compulsion which the capitals within it practice upon one another, on labor, etc. (the competition among workers is only another form of the competition among capitals), is the *free*, at the same time the *real* development of wealth as capital. So much is this the case that the most profound economic thinkers, such as, e.g., Ricardo, *presuppose* the absolute predominance of free competition in order to be able to study and to formulate the adequate laws of capital—which appear at the same time as the vital tendencies governing over it. But free competition is the adequate form of the productive process of capital. The further it is developed, the purer the forms in which its motion appears. (pp. 650–51)

Like the classical economists before him, Marx thus assigned to competition a very important, indeed an indispensable, role, that of enforcer of the laws of capitalism. But, again like the classics, what interested him were the laws themselves and not the means of their realization. He took for granted that competition would develop along with capitalism and the laws that competition enforces would become closer and closer approximations to reality. Given this perspective, there was no need for lengthy disquisitions on competition, and in fact Marx's comments on the subject were mostly incidental to discussion of other topics and often more concerned with earlier writers' misconceptions about the role of competition than with analyzing its workings.*

In this connection it is necessary to keep in mind not only that Marx's focus was on the laws of capitalism rather than on the means of their realization, but also that his concern was with the system's laws "of motion," as he explicitly stated in the Preface to the first edition of Volume I of *Capital*. For him competition could not be "perfect" or "pure," nor could it end in equilibrium situations lending themselves to analysis as to their uniqueness, stability, and so on. Fantasies of this kind were imported into economics only much later by those more interested in concealing than revealing the real role of the economy in shaping the history and destiny of bourgeois society. Neither Marx nor the classical economists had any interest in playing such intellectual games. For them, and for Marx most of all, competition was an elemental force, somewhat comparable to the force of gravity, which keeps the parts of the system in place and interacting with each other in intelligible ways.

Marx, of course, recognized that in practice the freedom of competition met with many obstacles and blockages, but he considered these to be leftovers from precapitalist social formations, which were in the process of disappearing with the development and spread of capitalist relations. He did not discuss the possibility that such barriers to competition might arise from the operation of the laws of capitalism itself. And yet, as noted above (p. 40), his analysis of the concentration and centralization of capital

---

*Volume 1 of the *Marx-Lexikon zur Politischen Ökonomie*, compiled under the direction of Samezo Kuruma of the Ohara Institute for Social Research of Hosei University (Tokyo) is devoted entirely to *Konkurrenz* (competition). It contains, apart from prefaces, appendices, etc., 359 pages, of which half are Japanese translation, in other words, about 180 pages taken from a wide variety of Marx's original texts. There are 176 separate passages, averaging just over a page apiece. And much of the space is taken up with providing the context of the remarks on competition rather than bearing directly on the subject. The *Marx-Lexikon*, of which eleven volumes had been published up to the end of 1979, is an invaluable source book and reference work.

and of the role of the credit system in making possible the creation of much larger units of capital than could be assembled by individual capitalists, obviously implied ongoing changes in the conditions of competition.

In the middle years of the nineteenth century, when Marx was gathering his material and writing the three volumes of *Capital*, the typical English industry, exemplified most clearly in the production of textiles, comprised hundreds of establishments each too small to influence the overall supply-and-demand situation and each striving with might and main to make a greater profit (or avoid a loss) through reducing its costs of production. "The battle of competition," Marx wrote, "is fought by cheapening of commodities. The cheapness of commodities depends, *ceteris paribus*, on the productiveness of labor, and this again on the scale of production. Therefore the larger capitals beat the smaller" (*Capital*, vol. I, chap. 25, sect. 2). Further, the credit system, which begins as a "modest helper of accumulation," soon "becomes a new and formidable weapon in the competitive struggle, and finally it transforms itself into an immense social mechanism for the centralization of capitals" (ibid.).

A consequence and bearer of these changes was the "formation of stock companies" (i.e., corporations) to which Marx devoted several pages in Volume III, Chapter 27, commenting on phenomena (like the separation of ownership and control) that bourgeois economics was to take account of only much later. The conclusions to which the analysis pointed are summed up in the following paragraph:

> This is the abolition of the capitalist mode of production within capitalist production itself, a self-destructive contradiction, which represents on its face a mere phase of transition to a new form of production. It manifests its contradictory nature by its effects. It establishes a monopoly in certain spheres and thereby challenges the interference of the state. It reproduces a new aristocracy of finance, a new sort of parasites in the shape of promoters, speculators, and merely nominal directors; a whole system of swindling and cheating by means of corporation juggling, stock jobbing, and stock speculation. It is private production without the control of private property. (*Capital*, vol. III, Kerr ed., chap. 27, p. 519)

In preparing this material for the press two decades later, Engels added a long editor's insert, beginning "Since Marx wrote the above, new forms of industrial enterprises have developed which represent the second and third degree of stock companies," and leading to the conclusion that "the long cherished freedom of competition has reached the end of its tether and is compelled to announce its own palpable bankruptcy." These new forms of enterprise were the cartel and what we know today as the holding company, i.e., a corporation that owns the shares of other corporations and in this way brings them under its control. As an example of the latter he cited the then recently formed United Alkali Trust "which has brought the entire alkali production of the British into the hands of one single business firm.... In this way competition in this line, which forms the basis of the entire chemical industry, has been replaced in England by monopoly, and the future expropriation of this line by the whole of society, the nation, has been well prepared."

As this last statement and similar remarks by Marx suggest, Marx and Engels did not see these changes as foreshadowing a new phase of capitalism but, in the words of Marx quoted above, as a "phase of transition to a new form of production," which they doubtless thought would soon come to occupy the center of the historical stage.

In the light of all this, it certainly cannot be said that Marx was unaware of the changing conditions of competition arising from the capital accumulation process itself. If, nevertheless, he did not inquire into the possible implications of these changes for capitalism's "laws of motion," there are at least two explanations which readily come to mind. One is that at the time of writing *Capital* (the early 1860s) these changes were still only beginning to appear and very little empirical material was available on which to base an analysis. And the second is that he saw the changes as basically symptoms of an impending transition from capitalism to a new form of production. Now, more than a century later, we know that he was too optimistic (most revolutionaries are likely to be). Not that the beginnings of such a transition were all that far in the future; it was only that they made their appearance first not in the historical heartlands of capitalism, but in the less capitalistically developed periphery of the global system. But even before this started to happen, the concentration and centralization of capital proceeded at an accelerating pace in the metropolitan centers of Western Europe, North America, and soon Japan.

With industry after industry falling under the domination of a few giant corporations, it could not but become clear to economists and other interested observers that the conditions of competition that had characterized the earlier stage of capitalism had been radically altered. Bourgeois economists began to deal with the new situation in a descriptive way even before the turn of the century, and an extensive popular literature of exposure and protest developed. In the United States Thorstein Veblen, who was much influenced by Marx but could not be called a Marxist, was the first social scientist to treat the subject theoretically (in his *Theory of Business Enterprise*, 1904); and the Austrian Rudolf Hilferding was the first to do so from an avowedly Marxist point of view (*Das Finanzkapital*, 1910). A few years later Lenin, who was much influenced by Hilferding's work, produced his *Imperialism, the Highest Stage of Capitalism* (written in 1916); and since then it has become a widely, if not universally, accepted tenet of Marxist theory that by the end of the nineteenth century the concentration and centralization of capital had proceeded to the point of transforming capitalism from its competitive stage, on which Marx had focused attention, to a new stage variously referred to as finance capitalism, imperialism, or monopoly capitalism.

The term "monopoly" recurs with great frequency throughout this literature, but almost never is it used to imply the exclusion or absence of competition. In this respect, the explanation offered by Veblen in *The Theory of Business Enterprise* would almost certainly have been approved by practically all the other writers referred to and by those who have continued to work in this tradition in later years. All producers, he said, are guided by the principle that, in the language of the railroads, is known as "charging what the traffic will bear." And he continued:

> Where a given enterprise has a strict monopoly of the supply of a given article or of a given class of services, this principle applies in the unqualified form in which it has been understood by those who discuss railway charges. But where the monopoly is less strict,

where there are competitors, there the competition that has to be met is one of the factors to be taken account of in determining what the traffic will bear; competition may even become the most serious factor in the case if the enterprise in question has little or none of the character of a monopoly. But it is very doubtful if there are any successful business ventures within the range of modern industries from which the monopoly element is wholly absent.* They are, at any rate, few and not of great magnitude. And the endeavor of all such enterprises that look to a permanent continuance of their business is to establish as much of a monopoly as may be. (New York: Charles Scribner's Sons, 1904, p. 54)

What is at issue in the transition from competitive to monopoly capitalism, therefore, is not at all the *elimination* of competition, but rather a change in the *forms* and *methods* of competition. In the earlier period when each individual firm supplied only a small share of the market, the main weapons of competition were lowering costs and improving quality: by such means the firm could hope to survive and increase its profits. The competition was not perceived as coming from particular rival firms that were also small and might enter or depart from the industry without noticeably affecting the market as a whole. Rather the competition was perceived as coming from all the other firms in the industry. In order to stay in business and grow, one had to do better than the average of all the other firms, for it was the latter that determined the value (or price of production) of the commodities being produced. Firms with costs above average would be squeezed out, those with costs below average would prosper. None could influence the market as a whole, either in terms of the commodities in demand or in terms of the prices at which they could be sold; all had to accept these as the givens of the situation.

As concentration and centralization proceeded, however, this situation changed. The number of firms in industry after industry

---

*At this point Veblen inserted the following footnote: "'Monopoly' is here used in that looser sense which it has colloquially, not in the strict sense of an exclusive control of the supply, as employed, e.g., by Mr. Ely [author of a book entitled *Monopolies and Trusts*].... This usage is the more excusable since Mr. Ely finds that 'monopoly' in the strict sense of the definition practically does not occur in fact."

(though, of course, not in all) declined to the point where each one supplied a considerable share of the market. The smaller the number of firms ("oligopolists" in the terminology of neoclassical economics), the greater the possibility for each one to differentiate itself from the others in significant ways and thus to add new dimensions to the competitive struggle. The key problem for a firm was to acquire a special position in a part of the market—through such methods as brand names, advertising and other forms of aggressive salesmanship, reciprocal favors to large buyers, and so on—and then to fight to fortify and extend its share. In this situation a firm conceived its competition as coming no longer from the industry as a whole, but rather from one or perhaps two or three firms nearest to it in the market. Competition, in other words, became much more visible and open and often much fiercer than it previously had been. In the early stages of this emerging mode of competition, there was a strong tendency for firms to try to improve their market position through price-cutting. Experience, however, gradually taught the lesson that this was usually a self-defeating strategy. Price-cutting could be as easily used to defend as to extend market share, with the only result being lower prices and profits for all contenders. In the closing decades of the nineteenth century, price-cutting of this kind was very widespread and certainly played an important part in bringing prices sharply down from the peak reached during the Civil War and its aftermath boom to a much lower level by the end of the century. With 1873 = 100, the wholesale price index fell to 53 in 1898 to the accompaniment of a steady stream of bankruptcies and loud complaints and cries of alarm from the business community, which experienced the period as one of almost unrelieved hard times.*

It was then that U.S. businessmen learned the self-defeating nature of price-cutting as a competitive weapon and started the

---

*It should be noted, however, that in terms of physical output, as distinct from prices and profits, the period was one of fairly rapid growth. Gross domestic product increased about threefold from 1870 to 1900, which compares favorably with any other three-decade interval for which estimates are available. See U.S. Department of Commerce, *Historical Statistics of the United States from Colonial Times to 1957* (Washington, D.C.: Government Printing Office, 1961), pp. 140–41.

process of banning it through a complex network of laws (corporate and regulatory), institutions (e.g., trade associations), and conventions (e.g., price leadership) from normal business practice.* In this respect the years around the turn of the century marked a watershed in the development of U.S. capitalism: the nineteenth century that, except for the Civil War period, was a century of falling prices gave way to the twentieth that, again with an exception for the Great Depression, has been equally notable for its rising prices.

The question we now have to ask is whether the transformation of competition brought about by concentration and centralization of capital negates the role assigned to competition by the classical economists and Marx, i.e., as the realizer and enforcer of the laws of capitalism. The answer is definitely not, and in one very important respect it is even true that this role is enhanced and strengthened. This is the case in the realm of relations between capital and labor. In the classical/Marxian scheme of things competition forces capitalists to produce at lowest possible costs, which of course is the other side of the coin of maximizing profits. This means that they will buy labor power as cheaply as possible and, having bought it, will squeeze out of it the maximum attainable

---

*The classic study of this whole process is Arthur R. Burns, *The Decline of Competition: A Study of the Evolution of American Industry* (New York: McGraw-Hill, 1936) an influential work in the late 1930s but one that has been almost totally ignored since World War II, a fact reflecting the ideological swing to the right of all the academic social sciences that was initiated by the Cold War and strengthened by McCarthyism. (Arthur R. Burns is not to be confused with Arthur F. Burns, the erstwhile chairman of the Federal Reserve Board.) It should be added that the banning of price competition has not been, and indeed could not be, complete. There are conjunctures in which an aggressively managed company with ample financial backing finds it worthwhile to deliberately incur losses in order to increase its market share, confident of its ability to raise prices and recoup when the dust of battle has settled. Still more important is the case of new industries (like electronics in the last two decades) in which the whole question of which of many small firms will survive and grow has yet to be decided. Here we have to do with a shake-down process that, in effect, repeats the experience through which many older industries had to pass many years earlier. These are exceptions that should not be allowed to obscure the truth of the dictum enunciated by the editors of *Business Week* when they wrote (June 15, 1957) that the price system "works only one way—up."

amount of production. This is a necessary, though not necessarily sufficient, condition for the validity of all the laws of value, surplus value, and profit. And the mechanism that produces it operates after as well as before the transition to monopoly capitalism. Capitalists are still forced by competitive pressures to produce at lowest possible costs. A weighty tome by a Harvard Business School professor explains why.* There are, according to the author, five competitive forces which "continually work to drive down the rate of return on invested capital toward the competitive floor rate of return, or the return that would be earned by the economist's 'perfectly competitive' industry" (p. 5). And in "coping with the five competitive forces, there are three potentially successful generic strategic approaches to outperforming other firms in an industry: (1) overall cost leadership, (2) differentiation, (3) focus." Of these the first is by far the most important. In Porter's words:

> Having a low-cost position yields the firm above-average returns in its industry despite the presence of strong competitive forces. Its cost position gives the firm a defense against rivalry from competitors, because its lower costs mean that it can still earn returns after its competitors have competed away their profits through rivalry. A low-cost position defends the firm against powerful buyers because buyers can exert power to drive down prices to the level of the next-most-efficient competitor. Low cost provides a defense against powerful suppliers by providing more flexibility to cope with input cost increases. The factors that lead to a low-cost position usually also provide substantial entry barriers in terms of scale economies or cost advantages. Finally, a low-cost position usually places the firm in a favorable position vis-à-vis substitutes relative to its competitors in the industry. Thus a low-cost position protects the firm against all five competitive forces because bargaining can only continue to erode profits until those of the next-most-efficient competitor are eliminated, and because the less efficient competitors will suffer first in the face of competitive pressures. (pp. 35–36)

There can thus be no doubt that survival and growth are as crucially dependent on minimizing costs as they were in the earlier stage of capitalism. But we can go further and say that in its ability

---

*Michael E. Porter, *Competitive Strategy* (New York: The Free Press, 1980).

to squeeze the most out of labor power, the giant corporation of today has greatly surpassed its small-scale ancestor. Here we can do no better than quote the leading authority on the subject, Harry Braverman, in *Labor and Monopoly Capital:*

> [T]he crucial developments in the processes of production date from precisely the same period as monopoly capitalism. Scientific management and the whole "movement" for the organization of production on its modern basis have their beginnings in the last two decades of the last century. And the scientific-technical revolution, based on the systematic use of science for the more rapid transformation of labor power into capital, also begins ... at the same time. In describing these two facets of the activity of capital, we have therefore been describing two of the prime aspects of monopoly capital. Both chronologically and functionally, they are part of the new stage of capitalist development, and they grow out of monopoly capitalism and make it possible. (New York: Monthly Review Press, 1974, p. 252)*

Marx considered that the "determining element" in all class societies—that which defines their fundamental nature—is "the specific economic form in which unpaid surplus labor is pumped out of the direct producers" (*Capital,* vol. III, chap. 47, sect. 2). Under capitalism this specific form is the capital/wage-labor relationship. The transformation of competitive into monopoly capitalism not only does not negate this relationship, it refines and perfects it. With respect to certain secondary characteristics of the system, most notably the distribution and forms of utilization of the unpaid surplus value, however, the transformation does bring about important changes, and this is why a specific theory of monopoly capitalism is necessary.

The altered forms of competition that prevail in monopoly capitalism create not the tendency toward a system-wide average rate of profit, which Marx analyzed in Part 2 of the third volume of *Capital,* but rather a hierarchy of profit rates, highest in the industries that approach most closely to a monopoly status and lowest in those in which small-scale competitive enterprise continues to

---

*See also Richard Edwards, *Contested Terrain: The Transformation of the Workplace in the Twentieth Century* (New York: Basic Books, 1979).

predominate. Since surplus value is distributed through the mechanism of profit rates, and since there is a rough correlation between the height of the profit rate and the number and size of firms in a given industry, it follows that there is a strong tendency, given a continuing process of concentration and centralization, for more and more surplus value to be sucked up from the smaller scale and more competitive sectors to the larger scale and more monopolistic ones. But since the amount of surplus value available for accumulation is always greater in proportion to the size and profitability of the unit of capital to which it accrues, it follows that the same total amount of surplus value will tend to support a more rapid rate of accumulation the more monopolistic is the overall structure of the economy.

Some of the implications of this for the actual unfolding of the accumulation process have already been briefly noted in the text above (pp. 42–43), and there is no need to repeat what was said there. But I do want to call attention to several points that have not been mentioned and that would require further exploration and analysis in a fuller treatment of competition and monopoly.

First, one should be careful not to freeze monopoly capitalist theory into the kind of rigid static molds that are the hallmark of neoclassical economics. When we say that the average rate of profit is superseded by a hierarchy of profit rates, there is no implication that the industries (or firms) at various levels of the hierarchy must always be the same. There is constant movement within the hierarchy in response to both internal and external factors. At the time of writing (early 1981) a particularly dramatic example is the reversal of the positions of the U.S. oil and automobile industries. A few years ago the automobile industry was on top by a wide margin, with oil at a considerably lower rung on the ladder. The sharp and increasing rise in the price of oil since 1973, together with sluggish adaptation to new conditions by the auto giants, has propelled oil to the top and plummeted autos to the bottom. Estimates appearing in the business press put the profits of the oil industry, dominated by a dozen or so huge corporations, at 30 to 40 percent of total nonfinancial corporate profits, clearly an unprecedented situation; while the three auto giants have been reporting the largest losses in U.S. corporate history. This relationship obviously will not last: oil will come down and autos will go up. But there is no guarantee that their relative positions will be restored to what they were before.

Similar, if less dramatic, examples could be drawn from the experience of many other industries. To which should be added that with the trend of recent years toward conglomeration, the relationship between firms and industries becomes increasingly blurred: most of the big oil companies are involved in petrochemicals and other forms of energy, and many are moving into mining; U.S. Steel, the biggest steel producer, is diversifying into chemicals, coal, oil, and gas; Armco, the fifth largest steel producer, already gets more than half its profits from energy-related operations, especially oilfield equipment; and so on and on. Since profits accrue to firms rather than to industries, the meaning of ranking industries by profitability becomes increasingly problematic. At the same time, however, the general proposition that the distribution of surplus value is increasingly skewed in favor of the larger units of capital is less and less open to question. And this is the heart of the matter as far as the relation between monopoly and accumulation is concerned.

Second, it is of more than passing interest to note that while Marx made no attempt to analyze the effect on the accumulation process of changing forms of competition, there is an intriguing passage very near the end of the third volume of *Capital* (in a chapter entitled "The Semblance of Competition") that suggests the direction his thinking might have taken if he had lived two or three decades longer:

> [I]f the equalization of the surplus value into average profit meets with obstacles in the various spheres of production in the shape of artificial or natural monopolies, particularly of monopoly in land, so that a monopoly price would be possible, which would rise above the price of production and above the value of the commodities affected by such a monopoly, still the limits imposed by the value of commodities would not be abolished thereby. The monopoly price of certain commodities would merely transfer a portion of the profit of the other producers of commodities to the commodities with a monopoly price. A local disturbance in the distribution of the surplus value among the various spheres of production would take place

indirectly, but they would leave the boundaries of the surplus value itself unaltered. If a commodity with a monopoly price should enter into the necessary consumption of the laborer, it would increase the wages and thereby reduce the surplus value, if the laborer would receive the value of his labor power the same as before. But such a commodity might also depress wages below the value of labor power, of course only to the extent that wages would be higher than the physical minimum of subsistence. In this case the monopoly price would be paid by a deduction from the real wages (that is, from the quantity of use values received by the laborer for the same quantity of labor [power]) and from the profit of other capitalists. The limits within which the monopoly price would affect the normal regulation of the prices of commodities would be accurately fixed and could be closely calculated. (*Capital*, vol. III, Kerr ed., pp. 1003-4)

While Marx has in mind in this passage only a "local disturbance in the distribution of surplus value," clearly the reasoning can be extended to encompass a more generalized spread of monopoly, i.e., of industries able to charge prices above price of production or value whichever is higher, and a continuing process of concentration and centralization. In addition to a redistribution of surplus value from more competitive to less competitive sectors, there could take place an increase in total surplus value at the expense of real wages (implying a rise in the rate of surplus value), if workers are unable to protect themselves against monopoly prices for wage goods. To this it might be objected that monopoly prices cannot raise the rate of surplus value except through depressing wages below the value of labor power, and that this would be essentially an unstable and temporary effect. This objection, however, fails to see monopolization as a process that must be viewed historically and as an ongoing part of the accumulation process. While at any particular time the value of labor power can be treated as a given, over a period of time it tends to rise (because of increasing costs of producing labor power and workers' struggles to improve their standard of living). In this context, growing monopolization must be seen not as depressing wages below the value of labor power but as slowing down the rise in the value of labor power. To this extent, it favors capital against labor by raising the rate of surplus value above what it would otherwise have been. It thus appears that two of the central ideas of the modern theory of monopoly capitalism—that the transformation of competition brought about by concentration and centralization of capital both raises the rate of surplus value and skews the distribution of surplus value in favor of the larger units of capital—are logical developments of a line of thought that Marx clearly adumbrated in the third volume of *Capital*.

The same cannot be said, however, of the other central thesis of monopoly capitalist theory, namely, that the changing size and composition of surplus value are accompanied by changes in the modes of utilization of surplus value, exemplified especially by the enormous growth, both absolute and relative, of selling costs in the last hundred years or so. In discussing the costs of circulation, Marx clearly established that these are deductions from the surplus value going to productive enterprises, and he thought of them as falling within the realm of merchant capital. Since there was thus a conflict of interest between industrial and merchant capital, and since the former was growing more powerful all the time, he thought that the tendency in the course of capitalist development was for the relative importance of the costs of circulation to decline. This was true enough in the period of competitive capitalism. But with the decline of price competition, other forms of gaining market share came to the fore, and these were heavily focused in the realm of salesmanship (product differentiation, branding, advertising, packaging, and the like). Some of these activities add use value to the buyer, but by far the larger proportion are concerned with salability pure and simple and are, therefore, for the most part to be treated as additions to the costs of circulation. Both the labor and the capital devoted to these purposes are unproductive (they consume but do not produce surplus value) and, therefore, from a social point of view, are to be accounted as sheer waste.

In the further course of development of monopoly capitalism, additional changes in the pattern of utilization of surplus value—notably those related to imperialism, militarism, and efforts by the state to counteract blockages in the accumulation process—emerged and grew steadily more important. In the second generation of Marxist theorists, these questions were placed at the center of inquiry by Hilferding, Rosa Luxemburg, and Lenin; and they have of course continued to preoccupy Marxists ever since. But in closing this brief discussion of competition and monopoly from a Marxist point of view, it is fitting that we should recognize that the first theorist to achieve a comprehensive vision of monopoly capitalism and its long-run consequences was the North American Thorstein Veblen. As early as 1904 Veblen delivered the following diagnosis, which rings truer today than it did three-quarters of a century ago:

> A disproportionate growth of parasitic industries, such as most advertising and much of the other efforts that go into competitive selling, as well as warlike expenditure and other industries directed to turning out goods for conspicuously wasteful consumption, would lower the effective vitality of the community to such an extent as to jeopardize its chances of advance or even its life. The limits which the circumstances of life impose in this respect are of a selective character, in the last resort. A persistent excess of parasitic and wasteful efforts over productive industry must bring on a decline. But owing to the very high productive efficiency of the modern mechanical industry, the margin available for wasteful occupations and waste-expenditures is very great. The requirements of the aggregate livelihood are so far short of the possible output of goods by modern methods as to leave a very wide margin for waste and parasitic income. So that instances of such a decline, due to industrial exhaustion, drawn from the history of any earlier phase of economic life, carry no well defined lesson as to what a modern industrial community may allow itself in this respect. (*The Theory of Business Enterprise*, pp. 64–65)

One may legitimately wonder, as we enter the last two decades of the twentieth century, whether this safety margin is not now at long last in grave danger of being used up. This is the question that lies at the heart of the crisis of our time.

[3]
CENTER, PERIPHERY, AND THE CRISIS OF THE SYSTEM

It is a commonplace these days that capitalism is in crisis: one hears it from friends as well as foes of the system. I believe that this is a defensible thesis, provided the meaning of the term "crisis" is appropriately clarified. It is basically to this task that I propose to devote this lecture.

First of all, it is necessary to be clear that we are talking about the overall capitalist system and not about a particular country or region. From the earliest period of its continuous existence capitalism has always transcended individual countries and regions, and by now it is a truly global system.

By speaking of the earliest period of capitalism's continuous existence, I mean roughly the fifteenth and sixteenth centuries in Western Europe. I do not mean to imply that there was no capitalism before then, or that capitalism could not have begun a continuous existence elsewhere. It will be useful, I think, to consider these two points somewhat further.

The earliest examples of what I would consider to be true capitalism emerged in a number of Italian city states during the Middle Ages. Of these, Venice was the earliest and a prototype for the others that came later. Venice's geographical position—offshore as far as the Italian mainland was concerned and strategically located for trade and conquest between the western and eastern halves of the Mediterranean—gave it a unique opportunity, of which it took full advantage, to develop an essentially bourgeois and antifeudal society that endured for many centuries. Trade, piracy, and tribute were of course the bases of Venice's great wealth; but its capitalism was not of a purely mercantile kind. Its shipbuilding and armaments industries, absolutely crucial to the society's very existence, were capitalistically organized and employed large numbers of wage laborers, and its political and cultural superstructure foreshadowed the bourgeois epoch to come, rather than reflecting the feudal context of its own time. A number of other essentially bourgeois city states flourished in other parts of Italy in the later Middle Ages; and in some, of which Florence was the leading example, a highly developed capitalist textile industry emerged with all the usual accompaniments of industrial strife and political class struggle. In the long run, these early sprouts of capitalism were too divided and weak to survive in a hostile feudal environment. But they did not succumb without leaving a rich legacy of economic practices (e.g., double-entry bookkeeping), political institutions, and cultural achievements which could be taken over and adapted to the needs of the Atlantic capitalist societies that emerged in the wake of the geographical discoveries of the fifteenth and sixteenth centuries and that finally established capitalism as the dominant world order for the next four centuries.

As for the possibility that a viable capitalism might have emerged in some part of the world other than Western Europe, it is obvious that this cannot be proved or disproved in any scientific sense. Yet it seems highly plausible to me: there were several regions with developed trading relations and money economies, necessary prerequisites to the emergence of a full-fledged capitalist order, and I see no reason to doubt that, given time, one or more of them would have achieved a breakthrough comparable to that which actually occurred in Europe. The point is that they were not given time. For a number of reasons, including the absence of a dominant centralized state, the situation in Western Europe was propitious, and the region got something of a headstart, two aspects of which were the development of superior technologies in navigation and firepower. These, in turn, enabled the Europeans to embark on a career of pillage and conquest that transferred vast amounts of wealth to their homelands and, at the same time, stunted or actually destroyed the development potential of possible rival areas. These rival areas, instead of undergoing an independent process of capitalist development, found themselves incorporated into the emerging Europe-centered capitalist system as colonies, dependencies, or clients of one sort or another. It was in this way that capitalism as we know it today started in its very earliest infancy as a dialectical unity of self-directed center and dependent periphery.

The fact that capitalism has from the beginning had these two poles—which can be variously described by such terms as independent and dependent, dominant and subordinate, developed and underdeveloped, center and periphery—has at every stage been crucial for its evolution in all its parts. The driving force has always been the accumulation process in the center, with the peripheral societies being molded by a combination of coercion and market forces to conform to the requirements and serve the needs of the center.

Owing to the overwhelming predominance of maritime transport and naval power, the early outward thrust originating in Western Europe affected mostly coastal areas of the other continents and nearby islands. This mode of expansion continued in later times but was supplemented, at first gradually and after the introduction of railroads on a much larger scale, by the penetration and conquest of huge inland areas and populations. What followed these successive waves of expansion was not everywhere the same. We can distinguish several more or less clearly defined patterns of action and reaction.

(1) Where precapitalist societies were weak and sparsely populated, the conquerors followed one of two possible courses. (a) They established new forms of production (plantations, mining compounds) using forced labor, both native and imported from other conquered territories. The products of these enterprises (gold and silver, tropical crops) were exported to the center and sold at enormous profits. The return flow of imports was made up of subsistence goods for workers, which could not be produced locally, plus luxury goods for resident Europeans. The exchange was of course vastly unequal and may be considered the prototype of all subsequent forms of unequal exchange between center and periphery. This was the pattern that prevailed in South and Central America, parts of South and Southeast Asia, and parts of Africa. (b) The conquerors wiped out or otherwise effectively eliminated the indigenous population and established settler societies more or less closely modeled on their homelands. North America and later

Australia and New Zealand were the leading examples. Where conditions were favorable, as in the United States, this type of settler colony soon developed ambitions for independent status and in time did in fact achieve independence and joined the nations at the center of the system as a rival and partner in exploiting the periphery.

(2) Where precapitalist societies were stronger and more highly developed, the Europeans sought to achieve their goals not by breaking up the existing order but by penetrating its power structure, playing off some chiefs and potentates against others, establishing effective overall colonial rule, and imposing on the local population both direct economic and indirect political forms of exploitation. India under British rule was the classic example of this pattern, but it was also widely practiced not only by the British but also by the Dutch and the French elsewhere in Asia, in parts of Africa, and in the Middle East.

(3) We come now to the final chapter in the story of European expansion, the encounter with Japan. Owing to a long history of relative isolation from outside contacts and to a geographical location that placed the country at the end of the road on which Western expansionism had embarked in Asia, Japan was a late target of the Europeans, who by that time had been joined by the North Americans in the race for empire. When the Westerners finally did reach Japan in the middle decades of the nineteenth century, they were slow to exploit their initial advantage, largely because of mutual rivalry and preoccupation elsewhere. This enabled the Japanese rulers, forewarned by the fate of other victims of Western expansion, to devise a successful strategy of maneuvering to preserve the country's independence while at the same time taking over from the West and imposing on Japan the social relations and institutions necessary to transform the country into a full-fledged capitalist power.

Within a remarkably short time (by historical standards), Japan passed from outside the periphery of the world capitalist system directly to the center. The route chosen—or, as some might argue, forced on Japan—was both historically unique and the only one that offered a chance of success. If Japan had allowed itself to be integrated into the periphery, it would have been trapped there, as literally scores of other countries have been. This would not necessarily have precluded rapid economic development, as the history of Brazil convincingly demonstrates. But development would have been dependent, not independent, and it never would have allowed Japan to reach the top echelon of the world capitalist pyramid.

This brings us to a crucially important question: What is the difference between independent development at the center and dependent development in the periphery? There are obviously many aspects to the question, but here I shall touch on only two of the most essential.

The first relates to the relationship between agriculture and industry. The heart of the matter was put in its briefest possible form by Samir Amin, a leading figure among Third World Marxists of the post-World War II period: "Unlike the countries of the center, where the 'agricultural revolution' preceded the 'industrial revolution,' the countries of the periphery have imported the latter without having started the former stage" (*Monthly Review,* July–August 1977, p. 16). Capitalism could never have put down roots in the center without a sustained increase in the productivity of agriculture and hence also in the agricultural surplus. This was the basis for the release of workers from the countryside; the flourishing of rural-urban trade; the emergence directly and through intermediate forms, like the putting-out system, of manufactures based on wage labor and embodying an increasingly elaborate division of labor; and only finally the introduction of machinery (the "industrial revolution") as the last step in ushering in full-fledged capitalism.

This is the only sequence that could have led to the development of independent self-sustaining capitalist societies. It is an illusion, perhaps widespread but reflecting ignorance of economic history, that industrialization somehow lies at the heart of the process of economic development. On the contrary, it is the final act and the crowning achievement of economic development; and there is no direct route to its successful realization, though of course countries like Germany and Japan, which were relatively late in embarking on the development process, could learn (as well as borrow) from their predecessors and in this way avoid mistakes and shorten the time required. But those countries that, to use Samir Amin's phrase, "imported" the industrial revolution without laying the necessary agricultural foundation have succeeded only in creating new forms of dependence.*

The second aspect of the difference between independent development in the center and dependent development in the periphery to which I want to call attention is simply this: the rate of exploitation is and always has been vastly higher in the periphery than in the center. In the center, the rate of exploitation is for all practical purposes the same as the rate of surplus value. This is not so of the periphery, where only a small part of the workforce is employed as wage laborers in capitalist industry, with a much larger proportion being exploited directly and indirectly by landlords, traders, and usurers, primarily in the countryside but also in the cities and towns. Here all or most of the surplus extorted from the workers not employed in capitalist industry is commercialized and becomes indistinguishably mingled with capitalistically produced surplus value. In these circumstances we can speak of a social rate of exploitation but should not confuse the concept with a rate of surplus value in the usual sense.

The high rate of exploitation in the periphery enables local ruling classes and allied elites to live on a level comparable to that of the bourgeoisies of the center, while at the same time making possible a massive flow of monetized surplus product (in the form of profits, interest, rents, royalties, etc.) from periphery to center.

---

*To avoid misunderstanding, it should be added that attributing to the countries of the periphery a failure to lay the necessary agricultural foundations for industrialization is not to deny that they have experienced certain kinds of agricultural development. The trouble is that these have centered on the cultivation of at most a few specialized crops for export, and in the process have tended to withdraw the best lands and other rural resources from vitally needed domestic production. The consequence is the paradox, almost universally observable in the periphery, of countries with predominantly agricultural economies unable to feed themselves and forced to import a large and increasing proportion of their requirements for grains and other staples from the countries of the center. This is why the first rule of a strategy for independent development in the periphery must be a determined move toward agricultural self-sufficiency, including food production. And this in turn means that industrialization must first and foremost be geared to the needs of agriculture.

The other side of the coin is a miserable, often bare subsistence or below, standard of living for workers, peasants, and the marginalized poor of countryside and urban slums. Well-meaning critics often deplore what they consider to be a drain of surplus out of the periphery that might have been invested in productive facilities catering to the impoverished masses, but this is to put the cart before the horse. The root of the problem is the high rate of exploitation, which both perpetuates poverty and at the same time prevents the growth of a mass market for consumer goods that would attract and justify investment in a local version of Marx's Department II. And, of course, the high rate of exploitation is built into the very structure of the system and protected by a formidable array of domestic and international institutional arrangements.

The counterpart of the very high (and frequently rising) rate of exploitation in the periphery is a lower (and over time relatively stable) rate of surplus value in the center. There are two basic and interrelated reasons for this. On the one hand, the working class of the center is more highly developed and is in a better position to organize and struggle for its own interests. On the other hand, the bourgeoisies of the center learned through historical experience that a situation that allows the standard of living of the proletariat to rise over time (a stable rate of surplus value combined with rising productivity) is not only functional but even indispensable for the operation of the system as a whole. Without it, the growth of Department II (producing consumption goods) is stunted, the demand for the products of Department I (producing means of production) is held down, and vitally important conditions for the operation of the capital accumulation process are absent. What this means is that a high and rising rate of surplus value, however desirable it may appear to be from the point of view of the individual capitalist, would be a disaster from the point of view of the capitalist societies of the center as a whole.

Nor is this all. In the early stages of the industrial revolution— up to the middle of the nineteenth century—the European bourgeoisies attempted, through anticombination laws and the like, to block the organization of the working class and in this way to boost the rate of surplus value. The result was the development of strong revolutionary currents in the newly emergent proletariat: not by chance was this the period during which Marxism, the worldview of proletarian revolution, was born and began the inexorable spread that has continued ever since. Alarmed by the revolutions of 1848, the ruling classes of the advanced capitalist countries began to reconsider their strategy, responding to the struggles of the workers more flexibly and discovering in the process that the new course paid both political and economic dividends. It was during the next half century that the modern labor movement, in its trade union and reformist political wings, took shape—against opposition that increasingly focused not on destroying the movement but on containing it within limits safe and even beneficial for capitalism. Soon after, as we shall have occasion to notice in due course, revolutionary Marxism began a "long march" from its birthplace in the center of the world capitalist system to the periphery, where conditions were—and are—more favorable to its development.

Corresponding to the contrast between the levels of exploitation in center and periphery is an equally striking contrast between the political systems in the two parts of world capitalism. In the center, by various routes and over a long period of time, bourgeois democracy became the norm and proved to be the political arrangement most conducive to the maintenance of a stable rate of surplus value and class relations reasonably compatible with the functioning of the accumulation process. In the periphery, on the other hand, efforts to copy the bourgeois democratic institutions of the center (very widespread, for example, in Latin America after the Spanish colonies achieved their formal independence and sought to model their constitutions on that of the United States) either produced empty facades or were discarded by dominant classes whose way of life depended on the maintenance of extremely high rates of exploitation and who saw in any concessions to the underlying population a dangerous threat to their continued rule. From the beginning, therefore, and now as much as at any time in the past, the norm in the periphery has been military-police states of one kind or another. They are, in fact, as closely related to high rates of exploitation as two sides of the same coin.

The implications of this analysis for the countries and peoples of the periphery are far-reaching. The extremely high rates of exploitation of which they are the victims are not, as conventional bourgeois wisdom would have it, a heritage of their precapitalist past to be overcome by the kind of policies prescribed in economics textbooks and touted by governments and international agencies like the World Bank—foreign aid and investment, transfer of technology, and so on, and so on. All such activities are carried out within the framework of the existing structure and normally have both the intention and the effect of strengthening rather than changing it.

Take, for example, the investment by multinational corporations in the periphery, which has occurred on a large scale in the period since World War II and has spurred the growth of modern industry beyond anything known in previous times. The multinationals, based in the advanced countries of the center, go to countries like Brazil—which is rightly considered a prototype of this kind of development—to supply and profit from markets that already exist and can be expected to grow with the general expansion of global capitalism. Some of these are domestic Brazilian markets fueled by the spending of perhaps 20 percent of the population in the highest income brackets. Others are international markets for agricultural products, raw materials, and certain kinds of manufactures, the costs of which can be kept low through the employment of cheap labor. But there is one market, potentially by far the largest, that does not exist and that the multinationals have no ambition to create, the market that would be generated by a rising real standard of living for the Brazilian masses. The reason for what at first sight might seem a paradox is simple: for capitalists, both Brazilian and foreign, the masses are looked upon as costs, not as consumers: the lower their real incomes, the higher the profits from selling to the local upper class and the international market. The dynamic at work here has produced a most startling result: in the fifteen years since the military coup of 1964, a period frequently referred to as that of the Brazilian "economic miracle," when the Gross National Product rose at annual rates as high as 10 percent, the level of real wages *declined* by a third or more. No wonder the president of Brazil on a visit to Washington several years ago was quoted in the press as saying, "In my country the economy is doing fine, but the people aren't."

The conclusion to which both theoretical analysis and historical experience lead is, thus, that for the vast majority of the peoples of the periphery, dependent development yields not a better life and a brighter future but intensified exploitation and greater misery. The way forward for them is therefore through a revolutionary break with the entire capitalist system, a road that is already being traveled by a growing number of countries in the periphery.

Against this background, and keeping in mind the analysis of the tendency to overaccumulation put forward in my last lecture, we can proceed to a diagnosis of the present crisis of the global capitalist system.

As always happens under capitalism, the seeds of crisis are sown in a preceding period of prosperity. In the case now under examination, this period can most conveniently be dated from the end of World War II. Listed in briefest possible form, the decisive results of that conflict were (1) the defeat of the Berlin-Tokyo axis; (2) the weakening of Britain and France; (3) the rise of the United States to undisputed hegemony in the world capitalist system; (4) the defection of China from the imperialist orbit; and (5) the maturing in the periphery of national liberation struggles with a consequent decline of traditional forms of colonial rule.

The period of undisputed U.S. hegemony lasted somewhat more than a quarter of a century, after which it began to weaken as the defeated powers of World War II gradually recovered their strength. The global capitalist system always works most smoothly when there is one undisputed hegemonic power, and the eroding and ending of that undisputed hegemony always signals the onset of a time of troubles and crises. In both respects the post-World War II period has run true to form.

Under U.S. hegemony, global capitalism had the benefits of a functioning and flexible international monetary system and a relatively free flow of international trade and capital movements. Gold and the dollar were established by the Bretton Woods agreements as interchangeable forms of universal money. The growth of trade and payments created a great demand for an increased supply of universally acceptable forms of money. The United States could and did satisfy this demand by running deficits in its balance of payments, thus pushing dollars out into the economies and banking systems of the rest of the world. For the United States this privilege was a source of enormous power, enabling the country to draw on the resources of the world almost at will. It was also a source of temptation and danger. The temptation was to abuse the privilege, the danger that abuse would wreck the system. As we shall see, the temptation was too great for the United States to resist.

But a workable monetary system and relatively free trade were not the only conditions favoring the accumulation of capital in the post-World War II period. The following must also be taken into consideration: (1) The need to repair the damage inflicted by the fighting and to make up for civilian shortages caused by diversion of resources to military production during the war. (2) The availability of an array of new capital-using techniques emerging from wartime developments (electronics, jet planes, etc.). (3) The enormous demands created by the military needs of the hegemonic power (and to a lesser extent its military allies).

These needs are inherent in the hegemonic position and have been greatly swelled by the special conditions of this period, especially (a) the emergence of the Soviet Union as a noncapitalist military/economic superpower, and (b) the spread of national liberation struggles and the efforts of the imperialist powers to defeat these struggles, involving two major regional wars (Korea and Vietnam) and many smaller military clashes. It is significant in this connection that the sustained postwar economic recovery of both Germany and Japan dates from the stimulus provided by the Korean war.

If we take full account of this historical setting, we can understand why the end of World War II opened up a period of unprecedented expansion for the global capitalist system. Ever since 1945 the upswings of the business cycle have been long by historical standards, the downswings short and shallow. The contradictions of the system seemed to have been so much reduced, if not actually eliminated, that they could realistically be thought of as a thing of the past.

But underneath the surface and mostly out of sight, certain long-term tendencies were at work that pointed to stormy weather ahead. The most important, I think, were the following: (1) overinvestment, (2) vast expansion of the debt structure, (3) weakening of the international monetary system, and (4) growing inequality between the center and the periphery. Let us look at each of these in turn.

Overinvestment. In the atmosphere of those years, optimism pervaded the business community in all parts of the global system. Capitalists built for a supposedly endlessly expanding economy. Enormous amounts of productive capacity were constructed, especially in basic industries like steel, shipbuilding, automobiles, heavy chemicals, and so on. Such an investment boom, as always, generates exaggerated prosperity in the short and medium runs, adding fuel to its own fire (expanding the steel industry requires much steel, and similarly throughout Marx's Department I). But as innumerable historical experiences have shown, this process cannot go on forever; and when it becomes clear that enough is enough, the letdown is likely to be all the more jolting.

Expansion of debt. This took place on an unprecedented scale both nationally and internationally. To quote from a special report on debt published by *Business Week* (October 16, 1978): "Since 1975 the United States has created a new debt economy, a credit explosion so wild and so eccentric that it dwarfs even the borrowing binge of the early 1970s." And internationally, a "massive flow of funds from the international market ... is enabling nations to keep rolling over old debt and taking on new debt nearly without limit." All this borrowing of course has sustained international demand and investment, but no one imagines that it can really go on without limit.

Weakening of the international monetary system. As noted above, the Bretton Woods system of equating dollars and gold gave the United States a unique power over the resources of other countries. For a long time this power was used in a way compatible with the maintenance of the system: deficits in the U.S. balance of payments were needed to supply the monetary needs of an expanding international economy. But the United States did not limit its creation of surplus dollars to this function. It used the power it had to shore up client regimes in the periphery, to maintain military bases around the world, to help finance the war in Indochina, and to expand its overseas investments. And in time these policies flooded the world with dollars on a scale far beyond the system's monetary needs.

By 1980, estimates of the amount of this dollar overhang amount to as much as $1,000 billion, sums far beyond the power of the United States to control, still less to liquidate. They are and will remain a sword of Damocles hanging over the head of the dollar. Since the near-panic selling of dollars in the month of October 1978, concerted efforts by major central banks have succeeded in maintaining a state of relative monetary calm. But the underlying situation did not improve and in fact seemed to be deteriorating as the United States led the developed capitalist countries into a renewed cyclical downswing. Attempts to unload unwanted dollars could resume at any time, with the ever-present possibility of a full-scale monetary panic. What the consequences might be we can imagine by going back to what happened after the last comparable incident, i.e., the collapse of the Austrian Creditanstalt in 1931 that triggered the end of the monetary system of the post-World War I period and initiated a new period of protectionism, currency blocs, and national controls over the flows of money and capital.

Growing inequality between center and periphery. The *fact* of growing inequality between center and periphery has been widely recognized and much commented on in recent years, though bourgeois social science has never provided a coherent, let alone convincing, explanation of it. For us, on the other hand, there is no mystery, and in addition from our point of view it is precisely when the capitalist system as a whole is expanding that the inequality can be expected to grow most rapidly. The explanation lies in the contrast between the relatively stable rate of surplus value in the center and the high and rising rate of exploitation in the periphery on which we have already commented. In a period of general buoyancy such as followed World War II, the center experiences rising real incomes for both capital and labor and a relatively high level of employment; whereas in the periphery, increases in income are concentrated in a small proportion of the population, while the producing classes suffer from declining standards of living and rising unemployment.

The consequence of all these coexisting, and largely interacting, trends and tendencies is twofold. In the center we observe a faltering of the capital accumulation process, renewed stagflation, and an out-of-control explosion of the debt structure. In the periphery the scenario includes declining standards of living for the masses, accompanied by increased political oppression; astronomical rates of unemployment, often reaching 30 to 40 percent of the labor force; misery, malnutrition, even starvation, with no let-up in sight and no improvement in prospect. Both parts of the global system are thus in a state of at least latent crisis, and signs that breaking points are being reached are not wanting—the near U.S. stockmarket and dollar panics of October 1978, the Iranian revolution, and, more recently, a wild, speculative increase in the price of gold, attesting to a distrust of *all* currencies. But apart from these specifics of the present situation, there is a much larger question at issue. The present crisis of the global capitalist system is shaped by forces that have been at work for more than a quarter of a century. They are still at work; in fact, they are inherent in the system. Unless something unexpected, like a major war, intervenes, they will continue to work. It is unlikely that they can be stopped or controlled by national governments, and there is no such thing as an international government.

[4]
MARXISM AND THE FUTURE

In my previous lectures I discussed the dialectical as opposed to the metaphysical mode of thought, capitalism and its development as a global system consisting of an autonomous center and a dependent periphery, and the crisis that now afflicts this global system. In this lecture I want to present a few thoughts on the revolutionary movements that have emerged to overthrow the system and the kind of societies they are creating where they have succeeded.

The fundamental ideas of Marxism date from the 1840s and are embodied in a series of works written between 1844 and 1848 by Marx and Engels singly or in combination: *The Holy Family* (Marx and Engels), *The Condition of the Working Class in England* (Engels), *The German Ideology* (Marx and Engels), *The Poverty of Philosophy* (Marx), and *The Communist Manifesto* (Marx and Engels). All reflect the overwhelming impact of the industrial revolution, which was then sweeping over England and parts of Western Europe. Like many of their contemporaries, Marx and Engels were deeply impressed by the rapid growth and the inhuman living conditions of the new factory proletariat described in great detail in *The Condition of the Working Class* and broadcast to the world in the *Manifesto*.

At no time in their later lives did they alter in any essential way the interpretation of the proletariat in the advanced capitalist countries and its revolutionary role, which they formed in that decisive period of their intellectual development. And yet the second half of the nineteenth century witnessed very significant changes in the living conditions and the political status of the Western Europe proletariat. The trend of real wages was up; working-class organization spread in both the economic and the political spheres; and welfare-state type reforms were won through continuing struggles (or in some cases conceded by ruling classes anxious to head off potentially revolutionary confrontations). These gains were made possible by the rapid expansion of capitalism, which set in after the failure of the revolutions of 1848, and by intensified imperialist exploitation of the periphery by the center in the last decades of the century.

Marx and Engels were of course not ignorant of these developments and indeed had ample opportunity to become acquainted with them at first hand through their contacts with English and European leaders of the rising working-class parties with which they maintained relations. But they failed to incorporate in their teachings the unavoidable conclusion that the working classes of the center, however potentially revolutionary they may have been in the early days of the industrial revolution, had been transformed by later developments into a reformist force seeking to improve the situation of their members within the framework of the capitalist system.*

That Marx and Engels were indeed correct about the revolutionary potential of the early industrial proletariat was demonstrated in a way that hardly any Marxists, brought up on the idea of the Western proletariat as the embodiment of revolutionary consciousness, could have anticipated, that is to say, by the Russian Rev-

---

*This is not to imply that the reformism of the working classes of the center, which developed in the second half of the nineteenth century and has persisted to the present, is a permanent feature of the global capitalist system. The century and a half in question has been a period of continuing, though uneven, capitalist expansion and rising real standards of living for the workers in the advanced capitalist countries. If, however, the argument of the preceding lecture is correct, that the global system has now entered a crisis phase that gives every sign of being irreversible, it is hard to avoid the conclusion that we are entering a new chapter in the history of the metropolitan working classes. It is of course much too soon to predict that this new phase will see a second transformation of these classes, this time turning them once again into a revolutionary force. But no Marxist should write off the possibility or renounce the struggle to bring about this outcome. It is becoming all too clear that the alternative is a descent into barbarism or, given the power of nuclear weapons, the self-destruction of the human race.

olution. The industrial revolution came late to Russia; but when it finally arrived toward the end of the nineteenth century, it quickly spawned a factory proletariat that was forced to live in and struggle against conditions similar to those that had existed in the West a half century earlier. This young proletariat, unlike its contemporary counterpart in the West, was highly receptive to revolutionary Marxism which, under Lenin's leadership, served as the indispensable guide to victory in the Revolution of 1917.

This was the first example of what was destined to become a general trend, the displacement of revolutionary Marxism from its birthplace in Western Europe to regions where conditions were more favorable to its taking hold and flourishing. The Russian Revolution itself played a crucial role in this process. Before 1917, Marxism had been largely confined to the developed countries of the center and their overseas offshoots—the composition of the First and Second Internationals demonstrates this very clearly— and, as already noted, by the time of World War I it had ceased, apart from its rhetoric, to be a revolutionary movement. After the Russian Revolution and the founding of the Third International, Marxism (now widely rebaptized Marxism-Leninism) spread throughout the periphery of the global capitalist system and increasingly became the ideology of serious revolutionary movements.

Here an important question arises: Are these twentieth-century revolutionary movements in the periphery proletarian in the sense that Marx and Engels and their early followers, including Lenin and the Russian Bolsheviks, understood the term? I think the answer has to be yes but with qualifications. They are unquestionably proletarian in the sense that the worldview and the ideology of Marxism that they have embraced were based on the experience of the proletariat created by the industrial revolution of the late eighteenth and early nineteenth centuries. Marx and Engels expressed the essential point in the following well-known passage from *The Holy Family:*

> Because the abstraction of all humanity, even the appearance of humanity, is practically complete in the fully developed proletariat, because the living conditions of the proletariat represent the focal point of all inhuman conditions in contemporary society, because the human being is lost in the proletariat, but has won a theoretical

consciousness of loss and is compelled by unavoidable and absolutely compulsory need ... to revolt against this inhumanity—all these are the reasons why the proletariat can and must emancipate itself. (*Werke*, vol. 2, p. 38)

It would hardly occur to anyone to write in this way about the working classes of the advanced capitalist countries in our time. And yet how can it be denied that it applies with full force to the dispossessed masses of the much more numerous and populous dependencies in the periphery of the global capitalist system? And is it not this basic similarity in the existential situation of the proletariat of Marx's time to that of the dispossessed masses of the periphery in our time that accounts for the remarkable fact that Marxism, starting as a specifically European phenomenon, has become more truly universal in its acceptance than any other body of ideas, secular or religious, in the history of humanity?

In this sense, then, the revolutionary movements of the periphery are certainly proletarian. But when it comes to the composition and leadership of these movements, matters are more complicated.

With regard to leadership, if the question is posed in terms of the class origin of the individuals who occupy the top positions responsible for shaping the theory and political practice of the revolutionary movements, then clearly it cannot be said that they are proletarian. But this was also the case in Marx's time and in Lenin's as well, and Marxist theory at no time expected it to be otherwise. In *What Is To Be Done?* Lenin put the argument in very strong terms that revolutionary theory and leadership could come only from outside the proletariat, but in this he was really only making explicit what was already implicit in the *Manifesto*. And certainly the experience of all nineteenth- and twentieth-century revolutions leads to the same conclusion.

But revolutionary leadership concerns much more than the individuals at the top. The entire body of activists who make up a revolutionary movement, including both cadres and rank-and-file militants, also play a vital leadership role in relation to the masses as a whole. Has their class character changed significantly with the displacement of the center of revolutionary gravity from the advanced capitalist countries to the periphery? If we may take the Russian Revolution as indicative of what a proletarian revolution would have been like in Western Europe if it had taken place before the rise of reformism, I think the answer is yes, a significant change has taken place with the shift to the periphery. The core of the movement that made the Russian Revolution was clearly recruited from the industrial proletariat, and it is even true that a significant part of the top leadership was from the same class. But this cannot be said of later revolutions which have triumphed in the periphery, of which the Chinese is by far the most important. That these revolutions took place under the banner of Marxism shows, as I have already argued, their proletarian inspiration. And in the case of China, the early growth of the Chinese Communist Party (CCP) took place in the big coastal cities and drew its support largely from their working classes, on the model of the prerevolutionary Bolsheviks in Russia. But after the defeats of 1927 at the hands of the Kuomintang and its foreign backers, the CCP was forced to retreat to the countryside, and thereafter right up to the final conquest of power two decades later, the composition of the revolutionary movement was largely rural (peasant, landless, petty bourgeois). This does not mean that there were no proletarian elements or that they did not play an important role, but they were certainly not predominant. And the same can be said, with variations of course, of the other post-World War II revolutions that have taken place in the periphery.

As to future revolutions outside the developed capitalist areas, there are a number of countries now, and quite likely there will be more in coming years, with industrial working classes that are small relative to the total labor force but that are employed in large-scale, technologically advanced production units and live under conditions reminiscent of an earlier period in the center—a situation somewhat similar to that which existed in prerevolutionary Russia. Here proletarian-led revolutions in the same sense that the Russian Revolution was proletarian-led are no doubt possible. But, in general, it seems more realistic to expect revolutions with a mixed-class leadership, the particular mixture in each case depending on the history and class structure of the country in question.

Before we turn to the question of what kind of societies these twentieth-century revolutions are creating, a few more words on the Russian case are called for. The fact that the industrial proletariat was the motive force for the overthrow of the tsarist regime and in this way made it possible for the peasantry to put an end to the landlord system in the countryside, does not mean that it was also the motive force behind the creation of the new postrevolutionary society. Perhaps the greatest tragedy of the Russian Revolution was the virtual destruction of the pre-1917 industrial proletariat in the bitter years of civil war and foreign intervention. A large proportion was killed in the fighting. Much of the rest left the cities with the onset of famine and the collapse of industrial production. Still others, surviving members of the party and the unions, were incorporated into the army or the governmental bureaucracy and cut off from their class roots. The new proletariat that emerged with the recovery of production and subsequent industrialization drives was drawn largely from the countryside and from declassed elements in the cities: from the beginning it had little in common with the proletariat that had made the revolution, and its further development took place under conditions vastly different from those that had shaped its predecessor. These are facts the importance of which has long been obscured by stereotyped, theoretical formulations and is only beginning to be appreciated by authors who now, in the perspective of more than half a century, see the crying need for a radical reinterpretation of Soviet history. (In this connection I will mention only the work of Charles Bettelheim, whose multivolume study *Class Struggles in the USSR* began appearing in 1974.) My purpose in raising this subject here is not to pursue it—that would lead us much too far afield—but simply to warn against uncritical acceptance of ideas that, because they have been around so long and repeated so often, have tended to acquire the status of self-evident truths. The Russian Revolution was indeed a proletarian revolution in the full Marxist sense of the term, but this carries no necessary implication about the nature of the society that emerged from it.

All postrevolutionary societies that proclaim their allegiance to Marxism (or Marxism-Leninism: I use the terms interchangeably) call themselves "socialist." The question I now want to raise is whether this usage is consistent with classical Marxism. In other words, are these societies socialist in the sense understood by Marx and Engels and Lenin, or is it now being used to designate a different reality?

The term "socialism" was used in a great many ways in the course of the nineteenth century, and the writings of Marx and Engels naturally reflect this variety of usages. I do not recall, however, that they ever defined it, directly or inferentially, as a particular form of society. In thinking about the present and the future, they focused on two forms of society, capitalism and communism, between which, Marx wrote in the *Critique of the Gotha Program*, "lies the period of the revolutionary transformation of the one into the other." The clear implication here is that the transitional society that exists during this period partakes of the nature of both capitalism and communism in varying proportions at different times, but is not and hence also cannot be conceptualized as a distinct society in its own right.

As a matter of terminology Marx dealt with this problem—again in the *Critique of the Gotha Program*—by speaking of the first and higher phases of communism. When Lenin wrote *The State and Revolution*, some four decades after the *Critique,* he felt free to substitute "socialism" for the first phase of communism on the ground that by that time this had become common usage. "And so," he wrote, "in the first phase of communist society (usually called socialism) 'bourgeois right' is *not* abolished in its entirety, but only in part, only in proportion to the economic revolution so far attained, i.e., only in respect of the means of production." Clearly Lenin was interpreting Marx, not disagreeing with him. For both of them the society to be brought into existence by a successful revolution, whether one chose to call it the first phase of communism or socialism, was by its very nature transitional and as such bound to be characterized by fundamental contradictions and conflicts.

Do the countries that nowadays call themselves socialist mean the term to be interpreted in the Marx/Lenin sense just explained? I cannot pretend familiarity with the theoretical doctrines of all of them, but so far as the Soviet Union and China, the two largest and most important, are concerned, the answer is definitely no, they do not see themselves as contradictory and conflict-laden societies in transition between capitalism and communism. They have not given up the ultimate goal of communism, but it no longer has an analytical or practical significance for them. They see socialism as a form of society in its own right—sometimes called a system, sometimes a mode of production—with laws of operation that are objective and discoverable in the same sense as the laws of capitalism. And in their view this form of society is definitely not characterized by antagonistic social or class conflicts. Official Soviet doctrine, for example, sees Soviet society (now called "advanced socialism") as consisting of two nonantagonistic classes (workers and peasants) and one stratum (the intelligentsia), presided over by a "state of all the people," and impelled forward toward communism by the "scientific and technological revolution."* The Chinese view has been moving in the same direction since the death of Mao Zedong, though it has not yet attained quite such a clearcut and neatly formulated expression.

It is quite clear that this theory of socialism as a form of society in its own right that is free of antagonistic contradictions and moved entirely by scientific-technological forces has no basis in classical Marxism, and amounts to a sweeping negation of the fundamental principle of historical materialism that class struggle is the motive force of history right up to the attainment of a classless and stateless communist society. This in itself would not be enough to condemn the theory: after all classical Marxism had no experience of postcapitalist society to build on, and projections based on the history of precapitalist and capitalist societies could conceivably be wrong. What is needed is not a comparison of Soviet-type theory with classical Marxism but rather of Soviet-type theory with Soviet-type reality.

When we undertake *this* comparison, we immediately encounter glaring discrepancies. The main problem areas concern the concepts and assumed roles of the intelligentsia and the state. In the Soviet theory the intelligentsia includes groups and individuals ranging from the politburo to the village school teacher, and in so doing it covers up crucial differences in their social status and functions. When we penetrate this mystification, we find that a large part of the intelligentsia consists of better educated and relatively privileged workers; an intermediate layer, which includes professionals, specialists, academics, artists, entertainers, and so on, who may

---

*See Pierre-Noel Giraud, "L'Économie Politique des Régimes de Type Soviétique," *Le Monde Diplomatique*, August 1978.

be highly paid but have little or no power; and a very small group who monopolize the top positions in the economy and politics (government and party) and make all the major decisions affecting the entire country. With respect to the state, the same kind of mystification is present. The only justification for calling it the "state of all the people" is that it owns most of the means of production, acting in legal theory as the representative of society as a whole. But this is a transparent fiction since the vast majority of the people have no control whatever, either individually or collectively, over the utilization of the means of production. Toward this vast majority, in fact, the state acts more as guardian or police officer than as representative or agent. All organizations to which significant numbers of people belong (e.g., the trade unions) are controlled from the top down, and the rank and file are denied even the most elementary rights of free association and discussion.

If we ask whether this kind of hierarchical and authoritarian society is also a class society, I think the answer has to be yes. Hierarchy as such is not proof of the existence of classes: if everyone at birth had the same chance as everyone else of ending up in a given position in the hierarchy, we could not speak of classes. But in practice hierarchies do not work that way. For many reasons that cannot be explored here, people born and brought up at a given level in a hierarchy tend to remain there: those at lower levels lack the means to climb to higher levels, and those at higher levels have the means to seek to rise even further or at least to resist being pushed down to lower levels. Naturally, in some institutional settings these advantages and disadvantages are stronger than in others, and they are especially strong where private property in the means of production prevails. But they always exist, and those who benefit from them can be counted on to do their best to strengthen them. This is why hierarchies that persist for any considerable period of time inevitably tend to develop into full-fledged class systems and can be prevented from doing so only by very powerful counteracting forces. Revolutionaries, including Marxists, have always tended to be sanguine about the possibility of changing these patterns of social behavior through revolution, one reason perhaps being that they are prone to confusing the destruction or far-reaching disruption of a given hierarchical system with the abolition of hierarchy as such, or at least of the forces tending to transform a reconstituted hierarchy into a full-fledged class system. The one revolutionary and Marxist who best understood these matters and sought to act accordingly was Mao Zedong. "Humanity left to its own devices," he told André Malraux, "does not necessarily re-establish capitalism ... but it does re-establish inequality. The forces tending toward the creation of new classes are powerful."* As we know, Mao did his best to see that in postrevolutionary China humanity was not left to its own devices: this was at the heart of many of the struggles within the Chinese Communist party after 1949, culminating in the Cultural Revolution. By now we also know that these efforts fell short of their goal and that since Mao's death China, following in the footsteps of the Soviet Union, has abandoned, at least for the time being, the struggle to counteract the forces tending toward the creation of new classes. The post-Mao leadership indeed, like its Soviet counterpart, seems to represent these forces rather than opposing them. The new-class-creating forces may have a long way to go yet in China, but the process seems to be well under way.

We return now to the question posed earlier about the kind of societies that are being created by the so-far successful twentieth-century revolutions. It seems clear to me that they constitute a form of society in its own right, which has to be contrasted to both capitalism and communism, and not treated as a transitional mixture of the two. To this extent their self-perception is valid. On the other hand, since they consider themselves to be Marxist, they must somehow reconcile this self-perception with the traditional view of Marxism that sees postrevolutionary society as a transitional stage and *not* as a social formation sui generis. At first sight this might seem an impossible task, like squaring the circle. How can postrevolutionary society be *both* a society in its own right *and* a transition from capitalism to communism? The answer is: *if the laws of motion of the postrevolutionary society are such as to lead automatically to communism.* Given this solution to the problem, the ideologists were entrusted with the assignment of inventing a theory

---

*Quoted in Victor Nee and James Peck, eds., *China's Uninterrupted Revolution* (New York: Pantheon, 1975), p. 108.

Marxism and the Future

of "socialism" (Lenin's name for the first phase of communism) that would fill the bill. And Soviet social scientists proved equal to the task, coming up with the theory already summarized of the nonantagonistic society propelled by the benevolent forces of science and technology.

Is it necessary to point out that this is not the first time a society, or at any rate its ruling class, has felt the need of a theory to cover up its antagonisms and present itself to its own members and the world at large as a beautiful blend of harmony and progress? What else, after all, has been the real meaning and function of neoclassical economics?

If these postrevolutionary societies are neither capitalism nor socialism in the classical Marxist sense, and are apologetically misrepresented by their own ideology, the question remains as to what they really are and how they function. And I am sorry to have to say that as far as I can see there are no very good answers from either bourgeois or Marxist social scientists. There is, of course, a good deal of descriptive material available, however, and I think it points to certain significant conclusions of which I call your attention to the following:

(1) The state, having taken over ownership of the means of production, becomes the central economic as well as political institution and not simply a complement to the private economy as under capitalism. For this reason we can call these societies state societies and their ruling class a state class.

(2) State societies are exploitative societies in the Marxian sense that those who do the work do not control their surplus product (either the way it is produced or the uses to which it is put).

(3) The production and utilization of the surplus product are integrated into the political process and are not governed as under capitalism by the mechanism of competing capitals (the heart of the Marxist theory of capitalism, briefly discussed in my second lecture) that drives toward maximum extraction and accumulation of surplus and in the process generates the characteristic contradictions of capitalism (business cycles, the reserve army of labor, polarization of wealth and poverty in both center and periphery but especially in the latter, degradation and dehumanization of work, etc.).

(4) The politicization of the surplus extraction and utilization process enables the state societies to achieve a kind of rationality (from the standpoint of their ruling classes) that is so strikingly absent from capitalism. Thus the first steps of a state society after its establishment are aimed at improvements in the living conditions of the masses (employment, health, education, social security), and these in turn serve to legitimize the society as such and (to a lesser extent) the policies imposed by its ruling class.

(5) Nevertheless, this process of legitimization has rather narrow limits. The monopolization of power and its attendant privileges (substantial even by capitalist standards) by a small ruling class necessitates the imposition of an authoritarian and essentially repressive regime, and absolutely precludes the development of genuinely democratic and self-liberating movements from below. To supplement repression as a means of maintaining control, the ruling class is thus increasingly forced into utilizing time-tested and (humanly) irrational methods such as consumerism and stirring up and playing on nationalist ambitions and passions.

(6) The basic driving incentive of capitalism—and this applies in greater or lesser degree to all classes—is fear: fear of unemployment, bankruptcy, loss of status, degradation, and not least (especially in the periphery), destitution and starvation. To the extent that state societies succeed in mitigating these all-pervasive fears without replacing them with more humane incentives, they create a void that manifests itself in what bourgeois ideologists perceive as inefficiency, irrationality in the allocation of resources, waste, and so on. From their own point of view, the most serious problem is lagging labor productivity.

If these are valid inferences from the facts as we know them about today's postrevolutionary societies, we are indeed dealing with a phenomenon that is historically new and that, given the rapidly deteriorating conditions in the periphery of the global capitalist system, seems almost certain to grow in importance in the period ahead. We therefore need to understand it better, and this I consider to be perhaps the most important task facing Marxist social science today.

Let me end by stating my own conviction that the spread and very real achievements of these societies have in no way lessened the relevance or importance of classical revolutionary Marxism for the future of humankind. State societies have eliminated or ameliorated some of the most disastrous and intolerable contradictions of capitalism. But they have also generated others, perhaps in the long run no less intolerable. They are certainly in no sense good societies, and their contradictions testify to their impermanence. Like capitalism, they too are producing their own gravediggers, in essence the same kind of deprived and diminished human beings Marx and Engels saw in the proletarians of their time. In due course, I have no doubt, these new proletarians will in their turn revolt against inhuman conditions, transform themselves from objects into subjects of history, and embark on a new adventure in creating a good society. When they do, they will, like generations before them, draw their inspiration from revolutionary Marxism.

Printed in the USA
CPSIA information can be obtained
at www.ICGtesting.com
JSHW021053060923
47929JS00002B/26